The Spanish-American War

Books in the America's Wars Series:

The Revolutionary War
The Indian Wars
The War of 1812
The Mexican-American War
The Civil War
The Spanish-American War

World War I
World War II: The War in the Pacific
World War II: The War in Europe
The Korean War
The Vietnam War
The Persian Gulf War

The Spanish-American War

by Deborah Bachrach

America's WARS

Lucent Books, P.O. Box 289011, San Diego, CA 92198-9011

Library of Congress Cataloging-in-Publication Data

Bachrach, Deborah, 1943–
      The Spanish-American War / by Deborah Bachrach.
            p.   cm. — (America's wars series)
      Includes bibliographical references and index.
      Summary: Examines the historical and political background of the
Spanish-American War, its major battles, and the ultimate effects of
the American victory.
    ISBN 1-56006-405-6
    1. Spanish-American War, 1898—Juvenile literature. [1. Spanish-
American War, 1898.] I. Title. II. Series.
E715.B12   1991
973.8'9—dc20   91-16730

To Bernie, for his love,
encouragement,
and insights

Contents

Foreword

War, justifiable or not, is a descent into madness. George Washington, America's first president and commander-in-chief of its armed forces, wrote that his most fervent wish was "to see this plague of mankind, war, banished from the earth." Most, if not all of the forty presidents who succeeded Washington have echoed similar sentiments. Despite this, not one generation of Americans since the founding of the republic has been spared the maelstrom of war. In its brief history of just over two hundred years, the United States has been a combatant in eleven major wars. And four of those conflicts have occurred in the last fifty years.

America's reasons for going to war have differed little from those of most nations. Political, social, and economic forces were at work which either singly or in combination ushered America into each of its wars. A desire for independence motivated the Revolutionary War. The fear of annihilation led to the War of 1812. A related fear, that of having the nation divided, precipitated the Civil War. The need to contain an aggressor nation brought the United States into the Korean War. And territorial ambition lay behind the Mexican-American and the Indian Wars. Like all countries, America, at different times in its history, has been victimized by these forces and its citizens have been called to arms.

Whatever reasons may have been given to justify the use of military force, not all of America's wars have been popular. From the Revolutionary War to the Vietnam War, support of the people has alternately waxed and waned. For example, less than half of the colonists backed America's war of independence. In fact, most historians agree that at least one-third were committed to maintaining America's colonial status. During the Spanish-American War, a strong antiwar movement also developed. Resistance to the war was so high that the Democratic party made condemning the war a significant part of its platform in an attempt to lure voters into voting Democratic. The platform stated that "the burning issue of imperialism growing out of the Spanish war involves the very existence of the Republic and the destruction of our free institutions." More recently, the Vietnam War divided the nation like no other conflict had since the Civil War. The mushrooming antiwar movements in most major cities and colleges throughout the United States did more to bring that war to a conclusion than did actions on the battlefield.

Yet, there have been wars which have enjoyed overwhelming public support. World Wars I and II were popular because people believed that the survival of America's democratic institutions was at stake. In both wars, the American people rallied with an enthusiasm and spirit of self-sacrifice that was remarkable for a country with such a diverse population. Support for food and fuel rationing, the purchase of war bonds, a high rate of voluntary enlistments, and countless other forms of voluntarism, were characteristic of the people's response to those wars. Most recently, the Persian Gulf War prompted an unprecedented show of support even though the United States was not directly threatened by the conflict. Rallies in support of U.S. troops were widespread. Tens of thousands of individuals, including families, friends, and well-wishers of the troops sent packages of food, cosmetics, clothes, cassettes, and suntan oil. And even more supporters wrote letters to unknown soldiers that were forwarded to the military front. In fact, most public opinion polls revealed that up to 90 percent of all Americans approved of their nation's involvement.

The complex interplay of events and purposes that leads to military conflict should be included in a history of any war. A simple chronicling of battles and casualty lists at best offers only a partial history of war. Wars do not spontaneously erupt; nor does their memory perish. They are driven by underlying causes, fueled by policymakers, fought and supported by citizens, and remembered by those plotting a nation's future. For these reasons wars, or the fear of wars, will always leave an indelible stamp on any nation's history and influence its future.

The purpose of this series is to provide a full understanding of America's Wars by presenting each war in a historical context. Each of the twelve volumes focuses on the events that led up to the war, the war itself, its impact on the home front, and its aftermath and influence upon future conflicts. The unique personalities, the dramatic acts of courage and compassion, as well as the despair and horror of war are all presented in this series. Together, they show why America's wars have dominated American consciousness in the past as well as how they guide many political decisions of today. In these vivid and objective accounts, students will gain an understanding of why America became involved in these conflicts, and how historians, military and government officials, and others have come to understand and interpret that involvement.

Chronology of Events

February 9, 1898
Publication of the de Lome letter.

February 15, 1898
Destruction of the *Maine*.

March 9, 1898

Fifty Million Dollar Bill becomes law; provides money to increase the size and strength of the army and navy.

April 11, 1898
President McKinley asks Congress for power to interfere in Cuban affairs.

April 21, 1898
United States declares a blockade of Cuba.

April 23, 1898
Spain declares war on the United States.

April 25, 1898
President McKinley issues call for volunteers to join the armed forces.

April 29, 1898
Admiral Cervera sails for Cuba.

May 1, 1898
Admiral Dewey defeats Spanish fleet in Manila Bay.

May 19, 1898
Admiral Cervera sneaks into Santiago Harbor.

May 26, 1898
United States learns that Spanish fleet is in Santiago Harbor.

June 14, 1898
American troops stationed in Tampa embark for Cuba.

June 22-26, 1898
American troops disembark near Santiago.

June 24, 1898
Battle of Las Guasimas.

July 1, 1898
Battle of San Juan Hill and El Caney.

July 3, 1898
Spanish fleet under Admiral Cervera destroyed outside Santiago de Cuba.

July 7, 1898
Congress votes to annex the Hawaiian Islands.

July 16, 1898
General Toral signs articles of surrender.

July 17, 1898
General Toral makes formal capitulation to General Shafter, and Spanish troops prepare to leave Santiago.

July 25, 1898
General Miles lands in Puerto Rico and takes control of the island two weeks later.

August 7, 1898
General Merritt issues ultimatum to Spanish in Manila.

August 12, 1898
Protocols of peace signed in Madrid.

August 13, 1898
Americans begin attack on Fort San Antonio Abad in Manila.

August 15, 1898
Spanish in Manila surrender.

October 1, 1898
Negotiations begin in Paris to end war.

October 28, 1898
President McKinley decides that the United States will keep control of the Philippine Islands.

December 10, 1898
Treaty of Paris signed by United States and Spain to end the war.

April 1, 1899
Treaty of Peace with Spain signed by the United States.

INTRODUCTION

"A Splendid Little War"

"A splendid little war." John Milton Hay, U.S. secretary of state, referring to the Spanish-American War.

Even though the Spanish-American War lasted only ten weeks and very few lives were lost, it was a significant event for the young United States. By winning the Spanish-American War, the United States proved to the world and to itself that it could and would fight against foreign nations, especially when those countries interfered in the western hemisphere, as Spain had done. In many ways, the war changed a relatively naive and isolated country into a world power.

For many years, world power had been concentrated in the countries of Europe. Nations such as Great Britain, France, Germany, and Spain had the most influence in global affairs. But a shift in power was gradually taking place as the United States matured. The young nation gained wealth and strength. Its population grew immensely, and many people believed it would become a major power.

Since its founding, the United States aspired to become a great power. In 1823, seventy-five years before the Spanish-American War, President James Monroe issued a bold proclamation. Called the Monroe Doctrine, it stated that one of the goals of the United States government was to prevent further European influence in the western hemisphere. This meant that the United States would fight to keep Europe from obtaining more colonies or from otherwise interfering in that part of the world.

At the time it was issued, however, the Monroe Doctrine was little more than an empty threat. The United States did not have the military strength or enough money or power to enforce the doctrine. But by 1898, this situation changed dramatically. The United States was then able to depend on a substantial military

Wounded Spanish prisoners at Brigade Hospital on San Juan Hill, Cuba, May 3, 1898.

force and growing international authority to enforce the Monroe Doctrine. And Spain would be the first country challenged by the United States.

Spain and Cuba

Spain was one of the European nations that had territory near the United States. Spain controlled some islands off the coast of Central America. The most important of these were Cuba and Puerto Rico. The United States believed that Spain misgoverned and abused the people of these islands. In fact, Spain did overtax and mistreat the Cubans, who rebelled in 1868 and again in 1895. The Spanish had put down these uprisings so brutally that the American people felt sympathetic toward the Cuban independence movements. At the time, Americans still felt the sting of British colonialism and immediately identified with other nations trying to throw off colonial rule.

In addition, Spain had frequently interfered with trade between its colonies and the United States. Even though the United States had been a trading partner with Cuba since the seventeenth century, Spain had sometimes stopped Cuban trade with the United States entirely. These actions caused serious damage to U.S. commercial interests. The United States disagreed with Spain's right to interfere with this trade relationship.

On March 22, 1898, the New York Journal *declares that "Nothing can justify postponing intervention in Cuba." One month later, the United States declared war on Spain.*

The United States was also concerned that other trading and commercial interests were threatened by the number of ships and soldiers Spain kept in the area. If the United States had to fight a war with Canada or Mexico, these Spanish forces could quickly mobilize against the United States. U.S. officials especially wanted Spanish troops out of Cuba because it lies only ninety miles off the coast of Florida.

Spain's Power Weakening

Over the years, then, the United States built up a great deal of resentment toward Spain, although it was unable to oppose such a powerful nation. At the same time, Spain's power was gradually weakening. Its economy had declined, and its military ships and weaponry were antiquated and in disrepair. Rapid political change toward the end of the nineteenth century further weakened Spain's power. Because political parties were attempting to overthrow its monarchy, the Spanish government was forced to devote many of its soldiers to defending the monarchy. As a result, there were fewer resources available for defending its far-flung colonies around the world. The stage was set for the United States to take a stand against Spain.

An illustration by W.A. Rogers in Harper's Pictorial History of the War with Spain *depicts the belief that the Spanish mistreated the Cubans. Here, Cubans are huddled outdoors, hungry and homeless.*

The U.S. defeat of Spain in the Spanish-American War forever altered the world status of these two countries. After the war, Spain became a relatively weak and unimportant country, and the United States was considered the dominant power in the western hemisphere. The United States succeeded in freeing Cuba from Spanish control. It also took over control of Puerto Rico, Guam, and the Philippine Islands from Spain. In addition, the United States gained the responsibility for governing and administering these islands. In ten short weeks, the United States went from having no international obligations to becoming a colonial power.

CHAPTER ONE

Spain, Cuba, and the United States

Spain and the United States mistrusted and disliked each other even before the United States became a fully independent nation. In 1775, Spain actively tried to strangle the young nation economically by cutting off its trade. For this reason and others, the United States naturally sympathized with the Cuban people as they began to break away from Spain in the nineteenth century. But the United States could do little more than sympathize. It did not have the power to fight Spain, and Spain showed no sign of giving up its control over Cuba.

Cuba was an important colony for Spain. The island's sugar, tobacco, and other raw materials were traded by the Spanish to generate great amounts of wealth. In addition, it became a matter of national pride for Spain to prove that it could hold onto Cuba, as it gradually lost many of its colonies during the nineteenth century. One by one, Mexico, Chile, Argentina, Bolivia, Peru, and other countries declared their independence. To ensure its continued possession of Cuba, large Spanish armies occupied it and kept the island under strict control. These armies brutalized the Cuban peasants to such a degree that Cuba rebelled against Spanish control in 1868. Called the Ten Years Revolt, this uprising led to much bloodshed on both sides.

Pedro Fardon was a Spanish officer serving in Cuba during the revolt. In 1869, he described Spanish soldiers' ruthless killing of Cuban farmers:

> Not a single Cuban will remain in this island, because we shoot all those we find in the fields, on the farms, and in

every hovel. We do not leave a creature alive where we pass, be it man or animal. If we find cows, we kill them; if horses, ditto; if hogs, ditto; men, women, or children, ditto; as to the houses we burn them: so everyone receives his due—the men in balls [bullets], the animals in bayonet-thrusts. The island will remain a desert.

Americans were horrified by reports of this bloodshed. When the Ten Years Revolt began, Ulysses S. Grant, the great Civil War hero, was president of the United States. He wanted to recognize the independence of Cuba but his secretary of state, Hamilton Fish, convinced him that the United States was too weak to support Cuba in a war with Spain.

Cuban Patriots in America

So although the United States did not openly fight Spain in 1868, it did nothing to prevent Cuban patriots from coming to the United States. These patriots recruited American soldiers and raised money to buy guns, ammunition, and boats to return to Cuba.

In the 1860s and 1870s, several of these joint expeditions set sail from Florida to fight against the Spanish army in Cuba. Unfortunately, none of the expeditions was successful. Most of the Americans who went to fight for Cuban independence were captured. Once captured, they were hanged by the Spanish.

Cubans burn plantations during the Ten Years Revolt.

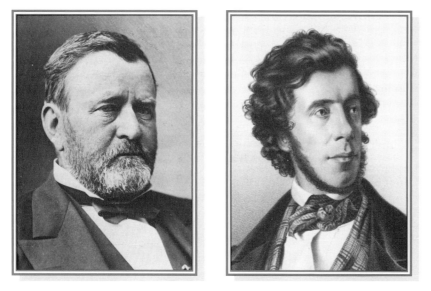

Secretary of State Hamilton Fish (right) convinced President Ulysses S. Grant (left) to stay out of the conflict between Spain and Cuba.

In 1895, Cuba again staged a major revolt against Spain. Conditions had not improved at all for the peasants. Many were starving, yet the Spanish authorities continued to increase their taxes to be paid to the Spanish government in Madrid. When Cuban peasants protested, they were brutally beaten.

One Cuban nationalist, Rafael de Eslava, described Cuba at the time of the rebellion in 1895:

> It seems to be self-evident that a curse is pressing upon Cuba, condemning her to witness her own disintegration and converting her into a prey for the operation of those swarms of vampires that are so cruelly devouring us, deaf to the voice of conscience, if they have any; it will not be rash to venture the assertion that Cuba is undone; there is no salvation possible.

Concentration Camps

The Spanish eventually sent more than 200,000 soldiers to Cuba to put down the 1895 rebellion and retain control of the island. At first, the soldiers were led by Gen. Arsenio Martinez de Campos. When he failed to crush the rebellion, the Spanish government replaced him with Valeriano Weyler, a general with a reputation for using harsh methods.

Weyler decided that he could contain the rebellion only by rounding up civilians and putting them in small areas that were guarded by Spanish soldiers. In a campaign called Subjugation or Death, an estimated 400,000 Cubans, mostly women and children, were placed in these camps without adequate food, clothing, sanitation, or medical care.

Concentration Camp

On October 21, 1896, Gen. Valeriano Weyler of the Spanish army decreed that he would begin a policy of concentrating people in small areas in fortified towns to stop them from assisting the Cuban rebels. Peasants were driven from their farms, and then their farms, crops, and livestock were destroyed. General Weyler hoped to eliminate a major source of supplies for Cuban guerrilla forces, which attacked his soldiers at night and then disappeared during the day.

Weyler ordered those people who refused to comply with the decree to leave their homes and move into the fortified towns. Weyler said that those who resisted would be "shot or hacked to death with machetes." The peasants who were driven from their farms were allowed to take with them only what they could carry on their backs.

As a result of Weyler's concentration policy, many thousands of Cuban peasants died of starvation and disease because the fortified areas were crowded and unsanitary. The people in the camps did not have enough food or water, and provisions for medical attention were lacking.

The mother superior of the Convent of the Sacred Heart in Havana, Cuba, described in detail the result of this campaign:

> The War is continuing its work of destruction. Captain-General Weyler's plan is to starve as many as he can and thus do away entirely with the Cuban race. He has succeeded in killing thus hundreds of thousands, without exaggeration, by the compulsory law of concentration. There are in this place over one hundred little children without fathers or mothers. Nobody takes care of them, and some die daily. A woman who had eleven children, has lost seven of them in three months and now she herself is dying.

A correspondent from an American newspaper reported to his readers about a method for disposing of the dead in Cuba in 1896:

> The dead cart is a great box on wheels, inside of which is another rough box which slides in and out like a coffin from a hearse. And indeed it is a coffin—the communal coffin, as it were—which those who are shot down in San Severino as well as those who die of small-pox in the pacifico settlements, and in which those who die of yellow fever as well as those who are found starved to death in the streets, are all laid and jostled during the mad gallop to the cemetery, or rather to the trenches adjoining the cemetery, where the dead are shoveled away out of sight under a few inches of sand.

Americans living in Cuba were not spared the horrors of the rebellion. The fate of some of these people is described by James Creelman, a reporter working for the *New York World* in 1896:

> No man's life, no man's property is safe. American citizens are imprisoned or slain without cause. American property is destroyed on all sides…. Blood on the roadsides, blood in the fields, blood on the doorsteps, blood, blood, blood! A new Armenia lies within eighty miles of the American coast.

Some Americans also became victims of General Weyler's concentration policies. About 700 to 800 Americans along with approximately 400,000 Cubans were rounded up and placed in the concentration camps. Many thousands of people, perhaps as many as 200,000, died in these camps from disease, starvation, and exposure.

Guerrilla Tactics

In retaliation for this treatment, the Cuban rebels burned vast areas of Cuba. They wanted to destroy Cuban sugar and the Spanish-owned tobacco plantations so the land would be useless and the Spanish would leave the country.

The Cuban rebels also selectively burned the property of Americans who would not give them money. Americans who could afford to pay for protection were spared. The American money was used to buy weapons and supplies to continue the revolution.

Rebel Leaders Seek Support

Rebel leaders hoped to gain the support of the American public for their cause. They thought the United States could drive the Spanish out of Cuba. So they sent Cubans to the United States to report to American newspapers the cruel acts being committed by Spanish soldiers.

Although both the Spanish and the Cubans committed atrocities, the American public heard only the rebels' side. This was because Spanish authorities would not permit American reporters near battle sites. So the only news Americans received came from the Cuban rebels. With their tales of oppression and patriotic zeal, the rebels stirred the desire of many young American men to fight on behalf of suffering Cuba.

As the revolt dragged on, the U.S. government tried to mediate between the Cubans and the Spaniards. In 1895, for example, President Grover Cleveland attempted to negotiate a settlement. He also tried to involve the other European powers in the process. But these attempts came to nothing, and the Spanish army tightened its hold on the Cuban civilian population.

In 1897, the conflict continued. President William McKinley, Cleveland's successor, sent his friend William J. Calhoun to Cuba to see if events were as bad as they had been presented in the American press. McKinley knew the American public was favoring a war with Spain over Cuba, and he wanted to know what was really happening.

Calhoun reported to the president that he had found Cuba "wrapped in the stillness of death and the silence of desolation." Calhoun reported that the great loss of life and property had not been exaggerated and that Cuba was slowly dying.

McKinley then also tried to negotiate peace. In 1897, he made an offer to purchase Cuba from Spain. The government in Madrid, led by its prime minister, Praxedes M. Sagasta, refused the offer outright. In a show of bravado, Sagasta told a Spanish newspaper reporter that his government would never "assent to foreign interference in our domestic affairs or with our colonies." Spain would rather fight than relinquish its hold on Cuba.

By 1897, the United States and Spain appeared to be at an impasse. Spaniards were incensed at U.S. attempts to involve itself in the affairs of Cuba, which the Spaniards believed to be part of Spain. Americans were furious that Spanish soldiers were locking people in concentration camps and sacrificing American lives and property in Cuba.

Many Americans believed the Spanish had violated the Monroe Doctrine, and they wanted their government to retaliate

Guerrilla Warfare

Guerrilla warfare is an irregular method of conducting war. This kind of fighting is characterized by frequent attacks by small groups of soldiers, usually operating without close ties to any kind of central military organization. Guerrilla warfare is generally used by small, poorly armed, but very dedicated irregular groups of fighters who are willing to risk their lives fighting against large, well-equipped regular army forces.

Spanish soldiers first used guerrilla tactics against the well-equipped troops of Napoleon Bonaparte during the Peninsular War of 1808–1814. The regular military techniques of the French were no match for the Spanish guerrillas, who succeeded in defeating Napoleon's armies and driving them out of Spain.

During the Cuban rebellion against Spain, rebels employed the techniques which the Spanish themselves had used so successfully against the French. They attacked trains (sometimes even unsuspecting Spanish garrisons) and stole arms and supplies. Then the rebels would escape retaliation by hiding in the mountains. The Spanish army, while better supplied and better armed than the Cuban rebels, could not fight an enemy they could not find.

Monroe Doctrine

In 1823, President James Monroe announced the Monroe Doctrine. The purpose of the statement was to tell the powers of Europe, particularly Spain, that the United States would no longer tolerate further colonization in the western hemisphere. The American people, it declared, were developing a political system different from the monarchical system in place in Europe. Any attempt to change the American democratic system would be regarded as "dangerous to our peace and safety," according to Monroe.

Curiously, the government of King George IV of Great Britain supported the American position. That was because in 1823 both Great Britain and the United States wanted to increase their trade with the newly independent countries of South America. Both believed that if Spain regained its lost colonies, new trade would stop. And this would economically damage both Great Britain and the United States.

In 1823, Great Britain had the strongest navy in the world. The American navy was tiny. The United States was therefore grateful for Great Britain's support and relied on the threat posed by the British navy to enforce the Monroe Doctrine.

At the end of the nineteenth century, the American navy changed. Ship construction improved, and steel replaced wood. The U.S. fleet rapidly developed into one of the strongest navies in the world. The United States could now enforce the Monroe Doctrine on its own. As the United States grew stronger, it not only wanted to keep further European influence out of Latin America but also wanted to eliminate the presence of European powers, such as Spain, entirely. The United States was determined to increase its own influence in Central and South America. In this way, the Monroe Doctrine took on meaning not originally intended by Monroe.

The United States used this interpretation of the Monroe Doctrine to justify its fight with Spain over control of Cuba. And again in 1962, the United States used the Monroe Doctrine to demand that the Soviet Union remove its nuclear missiles from Cuba.

President James Monroe originally developed the Monroe Doctrine to keep Europe out of the western hemisphere.

against Spain. Sen. Redfield Proctor of Vermont made a trip to Cuba in 1897 that seemed to confirm the need for U.S. action. On his return, he reported to the president and to Congress that he had found "the entire native population of Cuba struggling for freedom and deliverance from the worst misgovernment of which I ever had knowledge." Sen. Francis E. Warren most clearly expressed the appeal for the United States to become directly involved in the Cuban tragedy. He believed it was his country's humanitarian duty to end the bloodshed in Cuba:

> We, a civilized people, an enlightened nation, a great republic born in a revolt against tyranny, should not permit such a state of things less than a hundred miles off our own shores as that which exists in Cuba.

From 1895 to 1898, American political leaders tried to find a way of ending the 1895 rebellion without direct military intervention. But when attempts at negotiation failed, military intervention became a much more realistic possibility. In 1898, talk of war increased in Washington and in cities and towns throughout the United States.

One Wrong Move

With so much tension in the air, a war could easily be set off by one wrong move. It was important that high-level officials in both Spain and the United States make every effort to remain calm and to avoid antagonizing one another. Unfortunately, the reverse happened.

Enrique Dupuy de Lome was the Spanish envoy to the United States. In February 1898, he wrote a letter to a friend in which he portrayed the American president, William McKinley, in very unflattering terms:

> weak and a bidder for the admiration of the crowd, besides being a would-be politician who tried to leave a door open behind him while keeping on good terms with the jingoes of his party.

The letter was "stolen" and printed on the front page of a New York newspaper on February 9, 1898. The letter's appearance was viewed as the "scoop of the year" among the press corps. Certainly, it helped to intensify anti-Spanish and pro-Cuban feelings.

Enrique Dupuy de Lome was forced to resign because of his indiscreet letter. Despite the resignation, Americans were still buzzing with anger against Spain. Then, less than one week after the appearance of the de Lome letter, an event of far greater drama rocked the American public. That event would bring Spain and the United States perilously close to war.

William McKinley, U.S. president during the Spanish-American War.

CHAPTER TWO

The Sinking of the *Maine*

The moon hung low on the horizon of the Havana harbor. The evening of February 15, 1898, was a beautiful, calm night. It was the kind of mosquito-free moment the Cubans occasionally experience before the rainy season begins.

On that evening, Capt. Charles D. Sigsbee of the U.S. Navy sat writing letters in the cabin of his ship, the USS *Maine*. Sigsbee was a seasoned sailor. He had served with distinction during the American Civil War, and he had demonstrated great control under adverse conditions. That may have been the reason he was selected for his current post. Because his ship could be attacked at any moment by Spain, Sigsbee's assignment was an extremely dangerous one and required handling by an experienced naval commander.

Captain Sigsbee was very anxious on that evening almost one hundred years ago. He knew that relations between the United States and Spain were very strained. So Sigsbee confined his men to the ship and tried to anticipate events.

On that balmy evening, the captain feared that American citizens who lived in Havana might have to be rescued and taken aboard the *Maine*. He was also concerned that if his own ship and crew were hit by gunshots exchanged between Cuban rebels and Spanish soldiers, he might be dragged into the rebellion. Worse yet were his fears that the *Maine* itself might be directly attacked.

Sigsbee took many precautions because of these fears. He no longer permitted unescorted visits by Cuban sightseers to the *Maine*. Throughout the ship, he posted guards who would

Capt. Charles D. Sigsbee of the USS Maine.

sound an early warning in case of an attack. Sigsbee also unlocked the storerooms containing the ship's guns and ammunition. In case an attack did occur, he wanted his crew to be able to defend itself quickly.

The captain understood both the importance and the difficulty of his assignment. Sigsbee knew that President McKinley ordered the *Maine* to Cuban waters on January 25 to protect American interests in Cuba. In addition, McKinley wanted to make it clear that the government of the United States wished to be involved in settling the current crisis in Cuban-Spanish relations.

Sigsbee also knew, however, that McKinley wanted to solve the Cuban problem through diplomacy. McKinley was a man of peace, and he wanted to conduct American foreign affairs in a peaceful manner. In 1897 and again in early 1898, the American president sent diplomats to Europe to try to find a way to stop the fighting in Cuba and perhaps obtain Cuban independence through negotiation. Even Pope Leo XIII was called upon to assist in the negotiations between Spain and the United States.

In 1898, the United States was powerful enough to influence international politics. Officials were willing to speak out strongly against not only the mistreatment of American citizens in Cuba but also against the injustice of Spanish control over Cuba. If negotiations did not work, the United States threatened to use force against Spain to protect American lives and property.

The battleship Maine *sails into its final port, Havana harbor. Captain Sigsbee had orders to protect American interests in Cuba.*

The Maine *explodes in Havana harbor, February 15, 1898. The explosions were so powerful that the wrecked ship sank almost immediately.*

American Investments

The United States had a good deal at stake in the crisis. Many U.S. citizens lived and worked in Cuba. Some Americans had millions of dollars invested in the island's sugar economy. Other Americans were actually fighting side by side with Cuban rebels, and their lives were in danger.

So McKinley sent the *Maine* to Cuba as a message to Spain that the interests of the United States could no longer be ignored. The burden of responsibility weighed heavily on the shoulders of Capt. Charles Sigsbee. He knew that his ship was in a dangerous situation. He knew that his own actions might play an important role in the relationship among the United States, Spain, and Cuba.

As events unfolded, however, Captain Sigsbee became a victim and never had the chance to initiate events. At exactly 9:40 P.M., on the night of February 15, 1898, a massive explosion took place aboard the *Maine*. Then there was a second explosion. Tragically, the explosions occurred in the forward section of the ship, which was close to the living quarters of the enlisted men. Most of them had already retired for the night.

The doomed ship sank almost immediately. Of the 354 officers and men on board the *Maine*, 266 were killed by the blast. Many others suffered terrible injuries. It was certain that explosions had rocked the ship before it sank. The details surrounding the tragedy and who was responsible for it, however, remained a mystery.

There were many eyewitness accounts of what happened. Captain Sigsbee himself survived the explosion and was able to report his impressions. He wrote:

> I find it impossible to describe the sound or shock, but the impression remains of something awe-inspiring, terrifying, noise rendering, vibrating, all-pervading. There was nothing in the former experience of anyone on board to measure the explosion by.

Lt. Robert Hood reported:

> I was sitting on the port side of the deck, with my feet on the rail, when I felt a big explosion…. I immediately sprang behind the edge for shelter and saw on starboard side an immense amount of foaming water and wreckage and groaning men out there. I heard some groans forward and ran forward on the quarterdeck down the ladder and I immediately brought up on an immense pile of wreckage. I saw one man

The tremendous force of the explosions blew apart the steel structure of the doomed battleship.

there who had been thrown from somewhere, pinned down by a ventilator. We got him up just in time, just before the water rose over him.

Another officer wrote: "Three of us were sitting in the mess-room, when a heavy explosion occurred. We rushed on the upper deck and found that the vessel was on fire and sinking. All efforts were then directed toward lowering the boats and saving lives, but the *Maine* settled quickly on the bottom of the harbor, only her upper works remaining above the water."

A civilian sea captain, Sherman Vanaman of the schooner *Philadelphia,* was also in the Havana harbor at the time. He saw the ship blow up and then sink. Vanaman immediately reported that the explosions had come from an external source.

Attack or Accident?

For Vanaman and for many other excited Americans, that could only mean that Spain had deliberately placed a mine under the ship's bow. "If the United States didn't fight over this," boomed Captain Vanaman to anyone who would listen, "the whole country ought to be blown up."

Other explanations were not considered in the patriotic heat of the moment. It did not occur to people, for example, that a mine could have been placed by rebels hoping to involve the United States in a war against Spain.

When the first explosion took place, Captain Sigsbee believed that his ship was being attacked. He issued orders to his crew to go to battle stations to stop boarding by the enemy.

But the enemy boarding parties never appeared. After his mind began to clear, Sigsbee considered other possibilities. Perhaps he was mistaken about a Spanish mine. Perhaps he was even mistaken about the source of the explosion.

Captain Sigsbee knew that the *Maine* used bituminous coal as its fuel. Bituminous coal could explode by itself if a ship were not properly ventilated, and the *Maine*'s bunkers were, in fact, inadequately ventilated. Explosions caused by poor ventilation had occurred before in other ships similar to the *Maine*. This type of calm and thoughtful examination by responsible people might have led to consideration of alternative explanations for the explosion. War between Spain and the United States might have been avoided.

After the night of February 15, however, the American people's anger at Spain could be contained no longer. With the destruction of the battleship, the American people went wild. One commentator observed that there occurred an "extraordinary burst of public opinion to which...the President...would find no effective antidote."

Was There a Plot to Destroy the *Maine*?

At the time of its sinking and for many years to come, no one really knew what caused the destruction of the battleship *Maine*. But many people, especially Hearst, suggested it was part of a plot to hasten United States involvement in Cuba. The newspaper staff of the *Journal* devoted a tremendous amount of time and effort to provide its readership with "proof" of Spain's guilt. Artists drew pictures illustrating the placement of torpedoes under the ship's hull that could be detonated from the shore by means of an electric wire. These and other diagrams appeared in eight full pages of the *Journal* on February 16. The following Sunday, February 20, the *Journal* published an extra on the *Maine*. It provided many photographs of the ship as it lay wrecked in the harbor along with headlines which declared "How the *Maine* actually Looks As It Lies, Wrecked by Spanish Treachery, in Havana Bay."

William Randolph Hearst used inflammatory headlines and graphic drawings to insinuate that Spain was responsible for the Maine *disaster.*

The Sinking of the *Maine* and the Newspaper War

William Randolph Hearst had two reasons for supporting the war in Cuba. First, he wanted the United States to defeat the Spanish in Cuba. Second, he wanted to outsell his journalistic rival, Joseph Pulitzer and so gain first place among American newspaper publishers. He hoped that reporting the horrors of a bloody war would increase circulation and help him achieve his goals.

In order to get every scrap of news on the war, Hearst sent a large newspaper staff to Cuba. The sinking of the *Maine* provided him with the opportunity to report a sensational event in a very dramatic manner. The public's appetite for such news, especially after the sinking, was insatiable.

On the morning of February 16, 1898, the headlines of the *Journal* appeared in black and red. The newspaper demanded to know "Who Destroyed the Maine?" Hearst even offered a $50,000 reward for information leading to the disclosure of the guilty party. Apparently the newspaper tactics worked. Circulation on that day reached a new high of 1,026,624.

American Anger

Americans were furious that an American ship and its crew had been destroyed. They were outraged that the detestable Spanish had dared to commit such an act. Americans demanded that McKinley stop negotiating with the Spanish government and take steps to avenge the sinking of the *Maine*.

Few Americans were untouched by the wave of patriotic outrage that swept across the country. The public demanded revenge. One of the angry people in the United States in February 1898 was the young Theodore Roosevelt. He was assistant secretary of the navy when the *Maine* exploded.

Roosevelt was an extreme nationalist and believed that the United States should enforce the Monroe Doctrine of 1823 by actively driving out all European influence from the western hemisphere. Upon hearing of the sinking, Roosevelt immediately announced that the "*Maine* was sunk by an act of dirty treachery on the part of the Spaniards." The American people agreed with him and showed their fury by hanging stuffed dummies that looked like Spanish officials in many public places.

President McKinley now faced the most important decision of his administration. He was responsible for the safety of American lives and property in Cuba. How would he deal with this crisis?

He urged the public to withhold judgment on what had happened until the completion of an investigation. "My duty is plain," he said. "We must learn the truth and endeavor, if possible, to fix the responsibility. The country can afford to withhold its judgment and not strike an avenging blow until the truth is known."

McKinley immediately called together a navy board of inquiry to investigate the tragedy. The board reported its findings to the president on March 25, 1898. It announced that the explosion was caused by an external source, probably a mine. It did not blame anyone for placing the mine.

"Remember the *Maine*"

The findings of the report were almost completely ignored in the face of a national clamor for action. An unknown drinker in a New York bar captured the spirit of the moment. He raised his glass in memory of the *Maine* martyrs. "Remember the *Maine* and to hell with Spain!" he shouted. And the war cry "Remember the *Maine*" stuck. The phrase was used in headlines in newspapers across the country.

After the explosion, events moved quickly. On March 9, 1898, three weeks before the navy board of inquiry completed its work, Congress had already unanimously passed the Fifty Million Dollar Bill. This gave the president the authority to spend fifty

Theodore Roosevelt, assistant secretary of the navy when the Maine *was sunk.*

million dollars to prepare the army and the navy for a war that had not yet been declared.

The passage of the Fifty Million Dollar Bill reflected the unanimous belief that Spain had deliberately blown up the ship because of American sympathy for the Cuban rebels.

Under ordinary circumstances the sinking of a ship does not lead to war. But circumstances in 1898 were not ordinary. Spain and the United States had already been snarling at each other for more than one hundred years because of deep political and economic differences. However, Spain had always been the more powerful nation and its will had always prevailed. In 1898, a major shift in the balance of power took place between Spain and the United States. Americans began flexing their young muscles in anticipation of forcing Spain to bend to their demands. The American newspapers fueled these desires. Publishers printed sensational stories that strengthened anti-Spanish feelings and increased the public furor over the *Maine* explosion. The newspapers were largely responsible for creating an atmosphere in which war against Spain became acceptable to most Americans.

CHAPTER THREE

The Press

The American press played a major role in leading the United States into a war against Spain in 1898. Unlike the situation during World War I, World War II, or the Vietnam War, the American press was decidedly pro-war in 1898. The press aroused a nationalist sentiment to such a fever pitch that President McKinley came to believe that if he did not fight the Spanish, he and his political party would suffer. Other political leaders also felt they had to respond to the public pressure for war. As one political writer of the time noted, "Better that Spain should be ejected from Cuba than Republicans be ejected from Washington."

Jingoism

This uproar was stimulated by two giants of the American press world. During the entire course of the Cuban rebellion, from 1895 to 1898, two rival newspapers fought their own war in the United States to gain supremacy in the American newspaper market. Both were published in New York City, and both had enormous national circulation and influence. These newspapers used the events in Cuba as a backdrop for their own journalistic rivalry. By reporting events in Cuba in a biased, inaccurate, and inflammatory way, these newspapers led the American public to demand that the quarrel with Spain be settled through war.

The moment was ripe for a military spirit to seize the American people. It had been more than thirty years, a full generation, since the Civil War, which ended in 1865. As historian Gregory

Mason points out, people had forgotten the horrors of that bloody conflict, and many young men were eager to fight a war against Spain.

The Civil War had been an important national experience and continued to be a major topic of conversation in the United States at the end of the nineteenth century. Many young men, however, were tired of hearing about the exploits of their fathers and grandfathers. They wanted glory of their own. The Cuban crisis seemed to offer such an opportunity. So accounts of the war in the American press were read with great relish and accepted without question by many people.

There was yet another reason why the journalists of the period were so influential. In the days before radio and television, newspapers were the major source of news. Publishers exercised a tremendous amount of political influence. But newspapers did not attempt to adhere to a policy of objective presentation of facts. In the 1890s, it was common for a newspaper to report the editor's interpretation of the news. If the information was inaccurate or even false, it was rarely challenged by the public, who had little or no means to verify it.

Before the Spanish-American War, the press began to print any story it could find about events in Cuba. Whether or not the news was verified, it was presented as though it were completely true. Step by step, the press heightened the American sense of outrage at reputed Spanish brutality toward the Cuban rebels. After the *Maine* was destroyed and the American press reported it as a fiendish attack against the United States, American anger toward the Spanish was at its peak.

A group of soldiers poses during the Civil War. Thirty years later, young men relished the idea of following in the footsteps of these Civil War veterans. Many longed to take part in a new national conflict such as the war with Spain.

Jingoism

Jingoism is extreme nationalism or fierce devotion to the interests of one's own country. The word originated in the Basque region of northern Spain. Literally the word means "The lord of the high" It was most likely introduced by soldiers or gypsies and was used as a mild oath or expletive as in "by Jingo."

The word was first used in England during the Russo-Turkish War from 1877 to 1878 by those who wanted England to enter the war against Russia. It appeared in a popular London music hall performance in which the chorus sang: "We don't want to fight, but, by jingo! if we do, we've got the ships, we've got the men, we've got the money, too."

In the 1890s, many Americans expressed this same form of extreme nationalism. They wanted the United States to take over or control the entire western hemisphere, which is all of North and South America. They were called jingoes by their political enemies, and the name stuck. The jingoism of charismatic and forceful people such as Theodore Roosevelt and Henry Cabot Lodge made the movement more popular. Many critics of American expansion pointed to the Jingoistic spirit of the late 1890s as a force that led America to acquire unnecessary colonies.

William Randolph Hearst and his wife (left). Joseph Pulitzer (right).

The two men who were primarily involved in the press war were William Randolph Hearst and Joseph Pulitzer. These men, especially Hearst, became associated with a new, colorful but irresponsible approach to journalism known as yellow journalism.

William Randolph Hearst

William Randolph Hearst was born into a wealthy California family. He went to New York City and bought the *New York Journal* in 1896. When Hearst purchased it, the *Journal* operated much as newspapers do today. It reported stories only after their accuracy had been checked and prided itself on a fair, objective approach to news. It was also failing financially.

Hearst wanted to revive the *Journal*'s circulation and make his newspaper the most powerful in American politics. Another man, however, stood in the way of his goal. This man was Joseph Pulitzer, the owner of the *New York World*.

Joseph Pulitzer

The *World* was easily the dominant newspaper in the United States when Hearst arrived in New York City. It had the largest circulation of any newspaper in the country. It cost two cents a

William Randolph Hearst

American publisher William Randolph Hearst (1863–1951) went to New York in 1896 after great journalistic successes in California. With the assistance of family money, Hearst bought the *New York Journal*. He was determined to use every means available to boost the circulation of the newspaper. These tactics included the use of enormous black letters, colored paper, full-page editorials, illustrations, and colorful cartoons. The rivalry between Hearst and Joseph Pulitzer for supremacy in the newspaper world is one of the great stories of American journalism.

Pulitzer did try to compensate for his journalistic sensationalism by including excellent editorial pages in the *World*. Hearst made no such efforts to educate the masses or to adopt a particular social cause. He continued to use the techniques of yellow journalism both in the *Journal* and in the nationwide string of newspapers he bought.

In 1912, Hearst made a bid for the Democratic nomination for president of the United States. At the convention, the second largest number of delegates was pledged to him, but he lost the nomination to Woodrow Wilson.

William Randolph Hearst and Joseph Pulitzer were bitter rivals, constantly struggling with each other for newspaper supremacy.

Yellow Journalism

The term *yellow journalism* was first used in the 1880s to describe the journalistic techniques of Joseph Pulitzer to boost the circulation of his newspaper, the *New York World*. Yellow journalism is sensational reporting that exaggerates and distorts the news. Rather than presenting events with clarity and precision, yellow journalists arouse and sustain popular passion in order to increase the circulation of newspapers. Some of the new techniques developed by these reporters included bold headlines, catchy phrases, dramatic illustrations, and fictionalized eyewitness accounts of tragic events.

In the 1890s, William Randolph Hearst acquired the *New York Journal* and adapted Pulitzer's techniques in an attempt to beat Pulitzer at his own game.

The events associated with the Spanish-American War gave Hearst a special opportunity to test his skills. He was tremendously successful. The *New York Journal* eventually sold more copies than Pulitzer's paper. In addition to establishing yellow journalism in the United States, the methods of Hearst and Pulitzer played an important role in preparing the American people for war against Spain. This kind of reporting was also a key factor in sustaining the demand for the acquisition of colonies, which came in the wake of the war.

Big, bold headlines and sensational reporting characterized yellow journalism. These newspaper tactics helped form and incite public opinion against Spain.

Hearst advertised his own headlines on billboards to gain an edge in his press war with Pulitzer.

copy, and more than half a million copies a day were sold. This was an enormously large readership for the 1890s. And the number of subscribers continued to increase.

The *World* was so tremendously successful because of Pulitzer's journalistic methods. Pulitzer ordered his reporters to stretch and distort the news. His paper reported on the most sordid murders and elaborated upon details if they were particularly bloody or terrible. These stories kept circulation up. By using these tactics, Pulitzer proved that the public had an incredible and continuous interest in such matters.

Hearst decided to outdo Pulitzer. He was convinced he could make the *Journal* more popular than the *World*, and he used his family's fortune to do it.

One of the first things Hearst did was advertise. He placed ads on billboards, in his own paper, and on the backs of sandwich men who announced the virtues of the *Journal* from signs attached to their bodies as they marched in front of the newspaper's offices.

Joseph Pulitzer

Joseph Pulitzer (1847–1911) was a Hungarian Jew who came to the United States and became a famous journalist, newspaper owner, politician (he was elected to Congress by New York State in 1885), and philanthropist. He bequeathed a large portion of his self-made fortune for the establishment of the Pulitzer Prize. In his memory, the prizes have been awarded annually on the recommendation of the Advisory Board of the School of Journalism at Columbia University in New York in recognition of outstanding work in various areas of journalism and literature.

In the 1880s, American newspapers were beginning to use drama and sensationalism in the presentation of news stories. Joseph Pulitzer bought the failing *New York World* from Jay Gould in 1883 and turned it into an enormous financial success by using the techniques of sensationalism more than anyone had before. The newspaper appealed to mass audiences with its highly readable style.

Joseph Pulitzer used drama and sensationalism in his news stories. These tactics helped sway public opinion toward war with Spain.

But advertising did not increase Hearst's sales greatly, and Pulitzer still retained a comfortable lead in circulation. So Hearst resorted to other means. He offered huge salary increases to Pulitzer's leading reporters and managers, and they quickly snapped up the offers. Hearst also purchased the talents of artists and cartoonists who were widely used by the newspapers in the 1890s.

Still, none of these tactics gave Hearst the success he craved. But when events in Cuba began to become extremely violent, Hearst decided to use the Cuban rebellion to achieve his personal objectives. He would use special reports and special reporters to scoop Pulitzer on the war. Hearst believed he could use the war between Cuba and Spain to win his personal war with Joseph Pulitzer. Before Hearst was finished with reporting the Cuban events, his own mother was so horrified by the tactics employed by the *Journal* that she told her servants never to let the newspaper in her home.

There were numerous examples of Hearst's journalistic excesses. For example, Hearst openly disagreed with the stated policy of the U.S. government toward Cuba. When the United States refused to recognize Cuban independence in 1896, the *Journal* stated that it would do so on its own. The newspaper announced that Cuban citizens were independent and were "animated by the same fearless spirit that inspired the counsel of the patriot fathers who sat in Philadelphia on the 4th of July, 1776." This recognition had no value for the Cuban rebels, but Hearst's opposition to his own government's policy indicated how far he was willing to go to dramatize himself and his newspaper.

All of Hearst's information in 1896 was obtained from Cuban exiles living on the Lower East Side of New York City. These men had no firsthand information about Cuban events. Nevertheless, they became "reporters" for the *Journal*. Based on their "accounts," the *Journal* told the world that the Spanish had "roasted twenty-five Catholic priests alive" and had "resumed the inhuman practice of beating Cuban prisoners to death."

Hearst saw that his sensationalism attracted readership because the circulation of the *Journal* began to increase. So he decided to control all news relating to the events in Cuba personally. Each story written by a reporter was edited by Hearst. Since Hearst wanted the United States to go to war with Spain, he always edited the stories to place the Spanish in the worst possible light. The Spanish government soon refused all reporters permission to leave Havana to witness events firsthand. So the reporters made up stories, artists depicted them, and Hearst edited and published them in his newspaper.

It was Hearst who dubbed the Spanish general in Cuba "butcher Weyler" for the atrocities he was reported to have committed against Cuban rebels. The *Journal* called Weyler a "human hyena" and a "mad dog." Its description of the general was extreme:

Judge

THE SPANISH BRUTE
ADDS MUTILATION TO MURDER.

MAINE SAILORS MURDERED BY SPAIN

The Spanish were accused of using brutal tactics against the Cuban rebels. American newspapers took advantage of these allegations and portrayed the Spanish as treacherous brutes. Here, an ape symbolizing Spain is portrayed as being responsible for murdering Cubans and U.S. sailors.

> Weyler, the brute, the devastator of haciendas, the destroyer of families and the outrager of women…pitiless, cold, an exterminator of men…. There is nothing to prevent his carnal, animal brain from running riot with itself in inventing tortures and infamies of bloody debauchery.

The *Journal* told the American people that Weyler's soldiers "massacred prisoners or threw them to the sharks; dragged the sick from their cots, shot them and fed their bodies to the dogs."

Rebel Injustices Ignored

The outrages committed by the rebels themselves were seldom mentioned. Even if he had wanted to, Hearst could not have been evenhanded in his reporting. Much of the little inside information he had, he received from Cuban exiles. If he printed the Spanish side of the story, Hearst might lose his news sources because they were not at all sympathetic to Spain. Little by little,

Hearst's sensationalism increased the sales of the *Journal*. His tactics were working.

The stories that appeared in Pulitzer's *World* were similar in tone but never reached the *Journal*'s level of exaggeration and distortion. Both Pulitzer and Hearst endorsed the idea of a war between Spain and the United States in their newspapers. A reporter claimed that Pulitzer, in fact, had said that he "rather liked the idea of war—not a big one—but one that would arouse interest and give him a chance to gauge the reflex in his circulation figures."

Despite his increasing success, Hearst became restless. He had not yet beaten Pulitzer. Equally important, Hearst feared that a war between the United States and Spain would never happen. Hearst came to view the struggle between Cuba and Spain as a battle between light and darkness. He wanted the United States to assist the Cuban rebels in gaining independence from Spain.

So Hearst tried even harder to get the American public to support the war. To achieve this aim, he sent his best reporters and artists to Cuba to get firsthand accounts of unfolding events. It was important to have artists on location because in the 1890s

Hearst and Pulitzer had their own war. They each wanted to sell the most newspapers and used the events of the Spanish-American War to do it. This rivalry is depicted in a cartoon from the era.

THE BIG TYPE WAR OF THE YELLOW KIDS.

NEW YORK JOURNAL, THURSDAY, FEBRUARY 24, 1898.

DESPERATE WORK TO HOLD THE UNITED STATES SENATE IN CHECK.

ANNUAL INSPECTION OF NEW YORK'S FIGHTING SEVENTH REGIMENT.

The newspapers during the Spanish-American War could not reproduce photographs well, so they relied on hand-drawn sketches to illustrate the unfolding events in Cuba.

photographic reproduction had not yet progressed to the point where it could be regularly used for newspaper stories. Artists therefore frequently sketched the accounts being covered by the newspapers. Hearst sent Frederic Remington, the famous sculptor and painter of Western scenes, to Cuba. Remington was instructed to depict in graphic detail any atrocities that could excite the American public into supporting war.

Frederic Remington went to Cuba to draw the war firsthand.

Frederic Remington

A famous exchange took place between Hearst and Remington soon after the latter arrived in Cuba. The Spanish would not give Remington permission to enter the Cuban interior. He was unable to illustrate the horrors that Hearst wanted him to find. So Remington wired Hearst back in New York, "Everything is quiet. There is no trouble here. There will be no war. I wish to return."

Hearst's response has been immortalized. "Please remain. You furnish the pictures and I'll furnish the war."

In addition to gathering the news in extraordinary ways, Hearst also changed the appearance of his newspaper to make it more exciting to read. One of these techniques is familiar to modern readers, but it was shockingly dramatic and different in 1897. Hearst used huge block headlines. These bold headlines captured attention and held it. Hearst used this technique to create the war he seemed unable to find.

Frederic Remington and Yellow Journalism

In February 1898, Frederic Remington was ordered to draw pictures for a story regarding the Spanish search for three Cuban girls trying to get to the United States. The picture, which appeared in Hearst's *Journal,* showed a beautiful, demure, young girl standing naked and helpless as a rugged Spanish soldier pawed through her clothing. When the girls arrived in New York, they denied that they had been badly treated. The only factual information was that they had been searched, but only by a police matron. Remington's pictorial representation of the event, however, was the one that was remembered by the reading public.

Attention-grabbing stories on the front page did not necessarily have to match the facts, as long as they sold newspapers. Frederic Remington (left) was able to enhance these stories with lurid drawings. This sketch (above) of a woman being searched by the Spanish served to incite rather than inform the reader.

(left) John Sherman, McKinley's secretary of war. (right) Tensions flared as Spain was accused of boarding and searching American vessels, as seen in the February 13, 1897, Journal.

For example, on February 22, 1897, the *Journal* headlined a story with "SHERMAN FOR WAR WITH SPAIN FOR MURDERING AMERICANS." But there was no truth to the story. John Sherman, McKinley's incoming secretary of war, had never expressed such an opinion. Sherman denied he had ever made this announcement. But the story was not retracted, and the American reading public believed that John Sherman favored war with Spain. Nor was there any truth in another headline that read, "FLEETS OF THE GREAT POWERS BOMBARD THE CUBAN INSURGENTS." But the country had no way of disproving the story.

In 1897, Hearst used the personal story of a beautiful young Cuban girl named Evangelina Cisneros to rally support for the Cuban cause. Evangelina was a Cuban revolutionary who, along with her father, had tried to stir up groups of Cubans to oppose Spanish rule. Although she was only eighteen years old, she already knew her way around military encampments.

When Hearst first heard her story, Evangelina and her father were being held in the Recojidas prison in Havana. They had not yet been sentenced for their crimes. *Journal* reporter James Creelman discovered them in the prison. He and Hearst believed they had found the makings of a truly sensational story.

Hearst and the *Journal* tried to turn Evangelina into a modern Joan of Arc, the young, fifteenth-century French heroine who helped her country's army defeat the English at Orléans. Hearst hoped that people reading the story of Evangelina would praise her courage and compare her to the French heroine. The newspaper also tried to arouse sympathy by depicting the young Evangelina as mistreated by evil, brutal soldiers. Hearst's staff of artists provided pictures that left little to the imagination. The *Journal* wrote of:

> The unspeakable fate to which Weyler has doomed an innocent girl whose only crime is that she had defended her honor against a beast in uniform has sent a shudder of horror through the American people.

Through his newspaper, Hearst started a campaign to free Evangelina. The campaign enlisted the support of such socially prominent American women as Julia Ward Howe and Mrs. Jefferson Davis, the widow of the president of the Confederacy. Even Nancy McKinley, the mother of the president, supported the campaign.

These women were moved by stories like the one that appeared in the *Journal* on August 18, 1897:

> This tenderly nurtured girl was imprisoned at eighteen among the most depraved Negresses of Havana, and now she is about to be sent in mockery to spend twenty years in a servitude that will kill her in a year…. This girl, delicate, refined, sensitive, unused to hardship, absolutely ignorant of vice, unconscious of the existence of such beings as crowd the cells of the Casa de Recojidas, is seized, thrust into a prison maintained for the vilest class of abandoned women in Havana, and shattered in health until she is threatened with an early death.

American women responded to such appeals by collecting signatures on petitions to free Evangelina. These were sent to the Spanish government. They appealed to the pope on her behalf. In this way, important American women became involved in Hearst's attempt to bring on war between Spain and the United States.

A *Journal* reporter succeeded in helping Evangelina escape from the Havana jail. The reporter drugged the other women in Evangelina's cell as well as the immediate prison guards. She was then helped through a cell window, one of the bars of which had been filed and bent by her accomplices. At first she was taken to a house of a friend in Havana and hidden. Then she was dressed in boy's clothing and smuggled on a steamer bound for New York City, where she was greeted at Madison Square Garden. She was even received in Washington, D.C., by President McKinley.

Circulation Soars

Needless to say, these events were related in great detail in the pages of the *New York Journal*. The newspaper's circulation began to soar, but still not quite to the level of the *World*. Another disappointment for Hearst was that the reporting of this story did not cause war to break out between Spain and the United States, as he had hoped. Hearst was forced to resort to more extreme tactics. He became the embodiment of the slogan he himself had written for his paper: "While Others Talk, the *Journal* Acts."

Hearst hired a man to spy on the Spanish envoy to the United States, Enrique Dupuy de Lome in hopes that de Lome would do something embarrassing. He even paid bribes to have the Spanish envoy's private mail read. One letter written by de Lome to a friend and "obtained" by the *Journal* described President McKinley in unflattering terms. The *Journal* published the letter under the banner headline "THE WORST INSULT TO THE UNITED STATES IN ITS HISTORY."

The *Journal* also published an impolite cartoon on February 10, 1898, depicting an angry Uncle Sam telling de Lome to "git." It also said, "Now let us have action immediate and decisive."

Less than one week later, the *Maine* blew up in Havana harbor. Because Hearst had so openly supported war with Spain, rumors circulated that he played some mysterious role in the explosion of the ship. But no proof exists. What is certain is that one day after the horrible loss of American lives, the *Journal* announced to the world that Spain was responsible for the catastrophe.

The *Journal* screamed in huge headlines that it knew the guilty party. It told its readers the day after the explosion that "THE MAINE WAS DESTROYED BY TRICKERY." This theme was repeated day after day. The *Journal* announced that "THE WARSHIP MAINE WAS SPLIT IN TWO BY AN ENEMY'S SECRET INFERNAL MACHINE." This authoritative announcement was accompanied by a diagram showing where and how the mine had been placed for maximum effectiveness.

Irresponsible Writing

These stories were untrue. They all emerged from the imagination of William Randolph Hearst. Irresponsible writing such as this led one observer to say of Hearst that he "snooped, scooped and stooped to conquer." Edwin L. Godkin, editor of the very well respected journal *Nation,* denounced the *Journal's* exploitation of the *Maine* disaster. "Nothing so disgraceful as the behavior of these newspapers in the past week has been known in the history of American journalism," he wrote.

Indeed, the naval fact-finding board never did establish Spanish responsibility for the blast that destroyed the *Maine*. Almost

Like Hearst's Journal, *Pulitzer's* World *featured notoriously inaccurate and explosive headlines.*

eighty years after participants in these events died, an admiral and great naval thinker, Hyman G. Rickover, reviewed the mystery of the destruction of the battleship. In 1976, Rickover established that the explosion was the result of an internal blast caused by insufficient ventilation.

In 1898, these facts would not have mattered to an American public eager for war. Even if the truth had been known, it would have been difficult, if not impossible, to convince the American public that Spain was not responsible for the explosion. William Randolph Hearst had done his work well. He used sensationalism to arouse American support of Cuban rebels. When a very dramatic event occurred, he used it to help push the nation into conflict with Spain.

He also eventually won his personal war with Joseph Pulitzer. On the day that the *Journal* printed pictures of the deadly "infernal machine" that supposedly "destroyed" the *Maine,* the circulation of the *Journal* reached an unprecedented 1,026,624. Hearst found sleazy journalism to be profitable. And he outsold the *World.*

CHAPTER FOUR

Mobilizing for War

The destruction of the *Maine* and the resulting public outcry made war between the United States and Spain seem inevitable. Both governments began preparing for conflict. The Spanish government appealed to other countries for support because it was poor and weak after four years of fighting against the Cuban rebels. The Spanish government believed that if it fought the United States unassisted, it would lose both the war and Cuba.

Spain's attempts to gain allies failed. The European powers expressed sympathy for Spain, and they even made a mild appeal to President McKinley to avoid war. But the European powers made it clear that they would not get involved in a Spanish-American conflict.

They did not avoid involvement because of loyalty to the United States, however. In fact, most felt sympathetic to Spain. But many of the European powers had internal or external difficulties of their own in 1898. Most of them were involved in conflicts over territory in Africa or Asia. They could not afford to come to the assistance of Spain. Therefore, in a very vaguely worded joint note to President McKinley, the European powers stated, "The Powers do not doubt that the humanitarian and purely disinterested character of this note will be fully recognized and appreciated by the American president."

Clearly, Spain could not count on outside help to fight the United States. So it began feeble efforts to enter a war it had never expected to fight and now believed it could not win alone.

(above) The 25th Company of the Spanish army in 1898. (right) Cuban mortars perched high above Havana, at the fortress of El Morro.

Spanish Strengths and Weaknesses

The Spanish government already had an army of more than 100,000 men stationed in Cuba. The army had some strengths and many weaknesses. The Spanish army in Cuba did possess many veteran soldiers who had previous combat experience in the Cuban jungles. But the army also had many new recruits. These boys had been forced into service and had no wish to die so that Spain could keep the disease-ridden island of Cuba.

The Spanish army in Cuba also needed more supplies and ammunition to fight a war against the United States. But it was difficult for Spain to produce or purchase modern weapons. Spain was also thousands of miles away—it could send reinforcements only by ship. This meant that the Spanish navy would have to maintain control of the sea around Cuba to enable supply ships to unload their precious cargo. But the Spanish navy was in a state of great disrepair. Spain had not kept up with the recent and expensive advances in naval technology. The Spanish fleet did not have high-powered artillery or the complete steel plating of ship hulls. Spanish ships in 1898 had few efficient armaments, little ammunition, and incomplete crews.

Ships

Besides being antiquated, the serviceable Spanish Atlantic fleet was only one-third the size of the American navy. The Spanish fleet that sailed for the Caribbean included four armored cruisers, twelve old cruisers, five torpedo gunboats, three destroyers, three torpedo boats, and four gunboats.

Only a few of these ships and their men were ready for service in war. In addition to lacking men, the crews had had no target practice in more than a year because of ammunition shortages. The bottoms of half the ships had not been cleaned for a year. This meant that they could not travel at their intended speed. The ships also lacked sufficient trained personnel such as engineers and stokers, who were needed to keep the ships sailing properly.

Segismundo Bermejo, the equivalent of the U.S. secretary of the navy, ordered Adm. Pascual Cervera, commander of the Spanish Atlantic fleet, to make up for the deficiencies as best he could. But without funds and supplies, Cervera could do little to refit the Spanish navy.

Under these circumstances, Cervera was pessimistic about the outcome of a war between Spain and the United States. He shared his doubts with Bermejo on February 25, 1898:

> I ask myself if it is right for me to keep silent, make myself an accomplice in adventures which will surely cause the total ruin of Spain. And for what purpose? To defend an island which was ours but belongs to us no more, because even if we did not lose it by right in the war, we have lost it in fact, and with it our wealth and an enormous number of young men, victims of the climate and the bullets, and in defense of what is now no more than a romantic idea.

Admiral Cervera's gloomy predictions did not make Bermejo change his war plans. Cervera set sail for Cuba with his doomed fleet. He had orders to decline or accept battle as he saw fit.

The Navy

In contrast with the Spanish navy, the American navy was well-prepared for war in 1898. The people responsible for its development had been influenced by a book written by Alfred Thayer Mahan of the American navy. *The Influence of Seapower on History,* which appeared in 1890, stressed the idea that a country could not be considered a world power without a modern and well-equipped navy.

Mahan influenced the views of the under secretary of the navy, Theodore Roosevelt, and Roosevelt's friend, Henry Cabot

The U.S. Navy

During the Civil War, the U.S. Navy grew from 69 ships to a total of 629 ships. A large number of these were ironclad ships, which played an important role during the war between the North and the South. After the war ended in 1865, however, the navy began to decline. The country was much more interested in westward expansion than it was in naval expansion. Although American exports increased, most goods were carried by foreign ships. American wooden boats rotted, and the ironclads decayed.

This situation began to change after 1883. At that time, the American steel industry was growing rapidly. Simultaneously, Congress became interested in rebuilding the navy as a sign of the country's growing power. To protect the steel industry, Congress declared that only American products could be used for construction of this "new navy." The steel industry in turn encouraged the building of newer and better ships. Initially, money was made available for the building of four steel ships—the *Atlanta, Boston, Chicago,* and *Dolphin.* These ships were the beginning of the modern steel navy.

They were among the finest ships in the world. In the next decade, more of these steel ships were built in American navy yards. Their steel framework and heavy guns outmatched the old Spanish fighting ships during the Spanish-American War. American admirals George Dewey at the Battle of Manila Bay and William Thomas Sampson at the battle of Santiago virtually destroyed the fleets of Spanish admirals Patricio Montojo and Pascual Cervera in 1898.

The Boston, *1891. The* Boston *was made completely from American-made steel and came equipped with the most advanced weaponry available. She became one of the first ships of the modern steel navy.*

Henry Cabot Lodge worked hard to get congressional approval of the funds needed to create an all-steel modern navy.

Lodge, the powerful Republican senator from Massachusetts. Beginning in 1883, these men greatly accelerated the development of an all-steel navy.

The results of their efforts were seen in the fitness of the fleet that went to war in 1898. The U.S. Navy included five battleships, six monitors, two armored cruisers, eight protected cruisers, nine small cruisers, one ram, one dynamite gunboat, six torpedo craft, and ten gunboats. All these ships had been built especially for war service and were ready for battle in 1898.

In addition, a great deal of money was made available to increase this already large fleet. On March 9, 1898, Congress set aside fifty million dollars for war preparations. The Department of the Navy immediately began using part of its share of this money to increase naval readiness. It bought auxiliary craft, including yachts, fast steamers, and tugboats, which could be used in support roles during war.

The ships were ready for war. They were fully manned. The crews had fire practice every day. The ships' bottoms were cleaned regularly. The fleet had traveled all over the world, had tested its equipment, and had gained much experience at sea.

Apart from its size, the American fleet far outclassed the Spanish fleet in many other ways as well. Only nine American

Alfred Thayer Mahan

Alfred Thayer Mahan (1840–1914) influenced the development of the modern U.S. Navy more than any other individual. Mahan was himself a sailor who rose to the rank of rear admiral through an uneventful career as a line officer at sea. He went to the Naval War College in 1885 to teach, and it was there that he began work on his major book, *The Influence of Seapower on History*. The work was so significant that it was translated into many foreign languages, including German and Japanese. Mahan's theory about the vital importance of having a navy in order to be considered a major world power greatly influenced the development of the naval forces of both Germany and Japan.

Mahan used Great Britain for many of his examples of how naval strength was the major factor in maintaining a country's world status. He was received at court by Queen Victoria, and he was honored by both Oxford and Cambridge universities for celebrating the great role played by the Royal Navy in the development of the British empire.

Mahan was retired and living in Italy when the Spanish-American War broke out in 1898. He was recalled to serve on the Naval War Board in recognition of his great expertise in matters of strategy and because of the major role he had played in ensuring that the navy would be able to defend U.S. foreign policy decisions.

Alfred Thayer Mahan wrote the most influential book of his time on the importance of a navy. He maintained that a well-equipped navy was an absolute requirement for a country to hold world power.

Ships

The huge new battleships ruled the sea. The Texas *is pictured here.*

The battleship Massachusetts *served in the Spanish-American War.*

Battleship huge warship with the largest guns and the heaviest armor in a fleet. American battleships that served during the war included the *Texas, Massachusetts, Oregon,* and *Iowa*. Spain had the *Pelayo*.

Cruiser faster and more maneuverable than a battleship, with less armor and firepower. American cruisers that served during the war included the *New York, Brooklyn, Boston,* and *Baltimore*. Spain had the *Infanta Maria Teresa, Viscaya, Almirante Oquendo,* and *Cristobal Colon*.

Destroyer a small, fast, powerful, heavily armed warship with high maneuverability. Spanish destroyers included the *Furor, Terror,* and *Pluton*.

(below) The cruiser New York, *1899. (right) Destroyers such as the* Hopkins *were capable of moving fast and hitting hard.*

(above) The small but deadly torpedo boat Stilleto fires a bow torpedo. The small gunboats (right) protected the rivers, preventing enemy ships from moving inland.

Gunboat a small, armed ship usually used to patrol rivers. U.S. gunboats included the *Nashville, Wilmington, Helena, Marietta,* and *Vicksburg.* The Spanish used the *Don Jorge Juan, El Caney, General Lezo,* and *General Concha.*

Torpedo Boat a small, fast, maneuverable warship equipped with torpedoes and light guns. The United States used the *Somers, Gwin, Rodgers,* and *Talbot.* The Spanish used the *Ariete, Azor,* and *Rayo.*

Monitor an armored warship, or ironclad, with a low, flat deck and heavy guns fitted in one or more revolving turrets. U.S. examples are the *Amphitrite, Miantonomoh, Monadnock, Puritan,* and *Monterey.*

Ram a ship with a sharp metal beak on the prow used to batter or pierce enemy ships. The United States had the ram *Katahdin.*

(bottom left) The iron-hulled monitor Monadnock. The sharp beak on a ram (below) allowed the ship to pierce the hull of enemy ships.

The battleship Iowa *enters drydock. Local repair yards were a great military advantage for the United States during the war.*

ships, compared to thirty-two of the Spanish ships, were constructed before 1890, for example. This meant that, among other things, the American navy had very little exposed wood that could catch fire during an attack. The United States was also much closer to Cuba than was Spain. The United States had shipbuilding and repair yards close at hand. The U.S. fleet could also draw on support from American merchant ships. Spain had neither ship repair yards nor a merchant marine to assist in the war effort. In comparing the Spanish fleet and the American fleet in 1898, there was every reason to believe that the U.S. Navy would be victorious.

The Army

Unlike the navy, however, the American army was poorly prepared for war. In large part, this lack of preparedness was due to a historic dislike for maintaining a standing army. The experience with the British army during the colonial period made Americans believe that unless there was a war, there was no reason to maintain a strong military force.

As a result, the United States had only a tiny army located mostly in isolated posts in the West. Even those outpost units were undermanned. The regular army numbered less than 24,000 officers and men. It would have to be greatly increased to face an army of more than 100,000 Spanish soldiers in Cuba.

The American government was enormously successful in raising an army. The newspapers had whipped up such enthusiasm for war that there was no lack of volunteers. President McKinley issued two separate calls for troops. The quotas required to fill both these calls were met. In addition to white military units, four regiments of black soldiers and eight to ten thousand black volunteers participated in the war effort.

Before the end of the war, 128,000 American men had joined the army on a volunteer basis. The enthusiasm of the volunteers was so great that a remarkably high percentage of them even agreed to serve for two years, if necessary, to meet the national emergency.

Raising an army was easy. Training and equipping it, however, proved to be difficult. All the problems associated with having

Advertising for army recruits proved to be very successful, largely because of the overwhelming public support generated by the newspapers.

The U.S. Army

During the early history of the United States, Great Britain had used its army to dominate the colonies. The colonists were forced to house and to feed soldiers who threatened their way of life. The memory of the brutality of these professional armies permanently affected the attitudes of U.S. leaders.

This distasteful early experience affected the organization of the U.S. Army of the independent United States. The new nation maintained only a small regular army under the direction of the federal government and also a small number of state troops who were under the control of the state governors.

In times of danger, state and federal forces could be increased by calling for volunteer soldiers. These volunteers would defend their country during the emergency and then return to their regular employment. Americans believed that this arrangement would prevent the military from dominating the country.

This system did prevent the military from becoming too strong, but it also left the country vulnerable to attack and unprepared to meet an emergency. While European powers developed modern military techniques, including the establishment of a general staff that acted as the brain of the army, the American army remained essentially a frontier patrol. In 1898, President McKinley was forced to call for a huge number of volunteers to supplement the tiny regular army. Although the calls were successful, only an inefficient system existed to turn the raw recruits into trained soldiers. If the war had lasted a long time, those American recruits would have had to face seasoned Spanish soldiers who were accustomed to using brutal methods to control their enemies.

After the conclusion of the Spanish-American War, Congress almost immediately began writing legislation that would result in the establishment of a general staff for the army. The country had learned its lesson during the war.

The war brought volunteers from all over the country. These men are U.S. army staff and line officers from the 2nd Regiment Oregon Volunteer Infantry, 1898.

The secretary of war reviews troops at a training camp in New York.

only a small regular army began to emerge. To begin with, the American army was inadequately supplied. It did not have a routine system for obtaining such basics as tents, draft animals, bedding, wagons, food supplies, and uniforms, for example. Weapons, even inferior ones, were also in short supply. When the War Department was suddenly called upon to provide these items in large numbers, its supply system failed.

The army's regular contractors could not immediately provide the large numbers of supplies required. New contractors had to be located, bids had to be placed, and purchase decisions had to be made. Since the army was not well-organized and did not act quickly and efficiently, many soldiers suffered more from deprivation than from the consequences of conflict.

The army also lacked the special equipment necessary to fight in a tropical environment like Cuba. Many soldiers had only heavy woolen uniforms. Many did not have boots. Frequently, there was no bedding or netting to keep away the army of insects that attacked the troops as effectively as the enemy soldiers.

Food was a constant problem for the army in 1898. To alleviate this problem, the army experimented with a new kind of canned meat. The soldiers called it "embalmed beef." It made many of the troops sick, which led to widespread investigations of army contractors in 1899.

These difficulties did not result from a lack of funds. The Fifty Million Dollar Bill passed by Congress made available large sums of money for military purposes. Unlike the navy, however, the American army in 1898 was so poorly organized that it could not take advantage of the money.

An army training camp in Tampa, Florida. The new recruits soon discovered that the base was woefully underequipped.

Morale

In addition to these difficulties, serious morale problems developed between the regular army and the new enlistments. Most members of the regular army were either West Point graduates or Civil War veterans. They were disliked by the volunteer soldiers, who were based in the individual states and were called to serve in the army in 1898. As one young volunteer explained:

> For a self-regarding American of good family to serve as a private, corporal or sergeant under a West Point lieutenant or a captain is entirely out of the question. West Pointers seem fit to introduce a caste feeling between themselves and noncommissioned officers and privates that is unpleasant in the extreme.

The volunteers wanted to serve only under their own officers who were elected by their own men. They saw war as an adventure that they wanted to enjoy with their friends and neighbors. The volunteer units had little training and discipline and rebelled against the officers' attempts to teach them regular army routines.

The American government had to turn these volunteers and amateur officers into an effective army quickly. The army hastily set up training camps to accommodate the soldiers as they arrived from all over the country. Most of the training camps were in the southern states. The largest of these camps was located in Tampa, Florida. Tampa was selected because it was the port closest to Cuba. The selection turned out to be a terrible mistake.

In 1898, Tampa was a small, dusty, Gulf Coast town. It had inadequate facilities to deal with tens of thousands of men. Only one small railroad line led to the army campsite, for example. There was also a shortage of water, which made the lives of the soldiers uncomfortable and unsanitary.

All the problems associated with lack of training and lack of planning were revealed at the Tampa base. The single railroad line that led to the camp became clogged with men, equipment, and food. Distribution services were inadequate, and many soldiers went without food, equipment, or both. Soldiers in the camps suffered terribly. Because of the inadequate sanitary systems and lack of clean water supplies, many soldiers began to get sick with dysentery and typhus.

One of these soldiers described in his memoirs the training camp conditions:

> Disorder prevailed and it was impossible to learn anything regarding our future movements. Accommodations for lodging were poor and we were initiated in our soldier life by turning in on plank and cement floors with newspapers for coverings. The refuse from the thousands of animals and other insoluble debris of the camp added to the aerial and indirectly to the aqueous pollution.

The army could not remedy all of these difficulties in 1898. It was the good fortune of the United States that the Spanish army in Cuba suffered from many of the same problems. The two military forces were equally matched in their ability and inability to fight a modern war.

CHAPTER FIVE

The War in the Pacific

By April 1898, the president and the Congress of the United States were convinced that the government of Spain would not grant Cuba its independence. So on April 19, Congress passed a joint resolution demanding that Cuba be set free. President McKinley signed the resolution on April 20, and the next day, the U.S. Navy began to blockade Cuban ports. Spain declared war on the United States on April 23. The Spanish-American War had begun.

Two front pages from the Journal *in the days leading up to the war. The enormous type used to highlight the events of the war had never been used before.*

(above) President McKinley signs the resolution demanding that Cuba be set free. (right) U.S. volunteers board a transport headed for Cuba.

Theodore Roosevelt played a key role in these events. Long before the Spanish-American War began, Roosevelt and his supporters had dreamed of gaining an empire for the country. These men were imperialists and dreamed of gaining control of European colonies to increase the power and influence of the United States.

Imperialism

Unlike most Americans, however, Theodore Roosevelt did more than dream. Roosevelt knew the extent of Spanish island holdings both in the Atlantic and Pacific oceans. In particular, he was aware that Spain owned a large, rich chain of islands in the South Pacific called the Philippine Islands. He thought the United States should gain control of these islands because they were extremely productive agriculturally. They could also be very important strategically to the United States. Because they were close to China, they could provide a base for increasing trade.

But the Philippine Islands would be difficult to take from Spain. Like the Cubans, in 1898 the Filipinos were engaged in a revolt against Spain. As a result, a Spanish army of nearly sixteen thousand men under Gov. Gen. Don Fermín Jáudenes y Alvarez and a fleet of seven battleships under Adm. Patricio Montojo were in the Philippine Islands to suppress the revolt.

Imperialism

At the end of the nineteenth century, the European powers vastly extended their control of territory in Africa and Asia. This was done in order to increase their power, to gain control of war materials, and to have a place to sell the goods and services they produced. The control of other countries became a way to demonstrate a nation's importance. This trend was known as imperialism. By the time the scramble for land was complete, the entire continent of Africa had been carved up among the powers of Europe.

There were people in the United States who believed that their country should also participate in this process. They wanted to gain an empire. By 1890, the United States had expanded from the Atlantic to the Pacific Ocean. There was no more continental land to conquer. There were, however, some island territories like Cuba, the Philippine Islands, Puerto Rico, and Guam that belonged to Spain. Many people in the United States, driven by a desire for imperial greatness, wanted to seize those islands. Their influence played a large role in deciding that the United States go to war with Spain in 1898.

Col. Theodore Roosevelt was a fierce imperialist. His views on expansion of U.S. territories eventually helped him gain the presidency.

Although Roosevelt did not know it at the time, the Spanish forces were not as formidable as they appeared to be. Both Governor General Jáudenes and Admiral Montojo had asked Spain for reinforcements of men and supplies. But the government in Madrid was primarily concerned with Cuba. What few supplies and little money Spain had went to support the Cuban effort.

Roosevelt was not alarmed by the presence of the Spanish forces. Instead, he made his own preparations to seize the islands in case of war with Spain. Early in 1898, while he was still under secretary of the navy, Roosevelt got his big chance.

On February 25, Secretary of the Navy John D. Long decided to take an afternoon off from work. Roosevelt was in charge of the entire American navy for the afternoon. Roosevelt sent telegrams and messages in all directions to prepare the United States for conflict.

One of these telegrams went to George Dewey, who was then in command of a very small American fleet of six small battleships in Hong Kong. The telegram read: "In the event of a declaration of war with Spain, your duty will be to see that the Spanish squadron does not leave the Asiatic coast and then you will begin offensive operations in the Philippine Islands." When John Long returned to work the next day, he was furious with Roosevelt and recalled most of the messages. The telegram to Dewey, however, was not recalled, proving that both Long and the president agreed with Roosevelt on his directions to Dewey.

George Dewey

So on April 30, while most Americans were thinking about the war in Cuba, Dewey and his small fleet raced from Hong Kong to Manila Bay in the Philippine Islands.

Roosevelt knew that he could rely on Dewey. He had used his own influence to have Dewey placed in the Far East command. The sixty-one-year-old U.S. Naval Academy graduate was a Civil War hero with a reputation for making the most of opportunities. The "ruddy little Vermonter with frosty hair and mustaches" had an authoritative manner to match his reputation.

Late on the night of April 30, Dewey and his men prepared for battle. All exposed wood was ripped from the newly painted, gray ships and thrown overboard. Sailors checked their cannons and ammunition. All lights were turned off on the ships. The sailors of the Far Eastern fleet waited for orders.

Rear Adm. George Dewey's flagship Olympia *was the first American ship to attack in the Battle of Manila Bay.*

George Dewey

As a young naval officer, George Dewey (1837-1917) served with the famous admiral David Farragut during the Civil War. Dewey was greatly influenced by Farragut and always determined his actions by asking, "What would Farragut do?"

In 1897, through Theodore Roosevelt's efforts, Dewey took over command of the Far Eastern squadron. He was in Washington when he learned of his appointment.

In his usual thorough way, Dewey discovered that the fleet was low on ammunition, even for peacetime purposes. He made preparations to get ammunition for the fleet. Once he arrived in Hong Kong, he took special care to prepare the tiny fleet for battle in case of war against Spain.

The battle of Manila Bay, in which Dewey was victorious, did not decide the outcome of the Spanish-American War. But it made European powers think twice about intervening on behalf of Spain. The battle also came at a time when the location and battle worthiness of the main part of the Spanish fleet was still unknown by the United States. So the victory was a great morale boost to people on the East Coast of the United States.

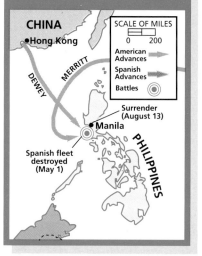

The Campaign in the Philippines

CHINA
●Hong Kong

SCALE OF MILES
0   200

American Advances →
Spanish Advances →
Battles ◉

Surrender
(August 13)
●Manila

Spanish fleet destroyed
(May 1)

PHILIPPINES

DEWEY
MERRITT

While they waited, Dewey pondered the situation. During the last week in April, he had received alarming information that the entrance to Manila Bay had been mined by the Spanish. According to these reports, the Spanish were also preparing to use torpedo ships to destroy the small American fleet. In addition, Spanish guns had been placed on the hills at the entrance to the bay, and the guns from Fort San Antonio Abad in Manila protected the Spanish fleet.

Even in the face of such obstacles, Dewey did not disappoint Roosevelt or the American people. As day broke on May 1, the American fleet, led by Dewey aboard his flagship, the *Olympia,* entered Manila Bay. Dewey decided to take a gamble and win or lose all in one head-on confrontation with the Spanish fleet.

"You may fire when ready, Gridley," Dewey told the captain of the *Olympia.* And the battle began. The outnumbered American fleet sailed into Manila Bay, the *Olympia* followed by the *Boston, Raleigh, Baltimore, Concord,* and *Petrel.* Their guns blazed away at the ships of Spain. Smoke and fire filled the air and the lungs of the opposing sailors. The bay resounded with the echoes of cannon fire.

It was an unequal fight from the start. The ships of Admiral Montojo in Manila Bay were in disrepair. The *Reina Cristina* with

The gunboat Concord, *one ship in Dewey's fleet used in the Battle of Manila Bay.*

The American fleet sails past enemy forts and through undersea minefields to attack the Spanish fleet hiding in Manila Bay. Even though the Americans were outnumbered, they completely destroyed the Spanish fleet. (below) The wreck of the Spanish flagship Reina Cristina, *sunk by the Americans during the Battle of Manila Bay.*

Admiral Montojo aboard, along with the *Castilla, Don Antonio de Ulloa, Isla de Cuba, General Lezo, El Caney,* and *Argos* fought bravely, but their efforts were doomed. The boilers of several ships were broken, and some could not even sail because their bottoms were covered with barnacles and debris. The Spanish ships were armed with old cannons, and the crews lacked proper ammunition and skilled marksmen. Their guns missed the American fleet almost entirely, firing either too short or too long. Some misfired, causing additional fires to break out on the wooden planks of the Spanish ships.

In an act of great bravery, Admiral Montojo broke away from his fleet and steered the *Reina Cristina* toward the *Olympia* in an attempt to destroy at least one of the enemy ships. His valiant efforts failed. The *Reina Cristina* received the fire of several American ships, which resulted in tremendous damage and great loss of life on the Spanish flagship.

Spanish prisoners gather around the noonday meal in Manila. Admiral Dewey's forces were able to capture 250 Spanish during the Battle of Manila Bay.

Maj. Gen. Wesley Merritt (seated, center). The defeat of the Spanish fleet at Manila Bay left the Philippines open to Merritt's conquering forces.

When the battle ended, the seven Spanish ships were on fire, had sunk, or were sinking. Almost four hundred Spanish sailors lost their lives in the battle. Many more were wounded.

Dewey had not lost a single man in battle, and his fleet sustained little damage. In all, two American officers and six men were slightly wounded on the *Baltimore;* one man was grazed on the *Boston;* and two men were slightly injured on the *Olympia.*

After gaining victory, George Dewey showed his true generosity of spirit. He wired to the president, "I am assisting in protecting the Spanish sick and wounded. Two hundred and fifty sick and wounded are in hospital within our lines."

Thus ended the Battle of Manila Bay. George Dewey had destroyed the Spanish fleet of Admiral Montojo and was the victor in one of the greatest sea battles in American naval history.

The victory at sea set the stage for the land battle to conquer the Philippines. Dewey spent the next two months making repairs on his ships and preparing them to assist the American army forces, which began to arrive in the Philippines in late June 1898.

Wesley Merritt

Maj. Gen. Wesley Merritt (1836–1910) graduated from West Point Military Academy and served with honor during the Civil War. He was promoted to major as a result of the bravery he displayed at the Battle of Gettysburg. Merritt was assigned to frontier duty after the Civil War. He became superintendent of West Point in 1882. In 1898, he was selected to lead what came to be called the Eighth Army. The Eighth Army was sent to the Philippine Islands to defeat the Spanish forces that controlled the colony.

General Merritt showed great tact and political skill in dealing with the Spanish army officers in the Philippine Islands. As a result, he was sent to France to assist the American commissioners who were negotiating with the Spanish.

A young Wesley Merritt during the Civil War era. His bravery during the Civil War was rewarded with recognition and rapid advancement. During the Spanish-American War, he was given the task of defeating the Spanish army in the Philippines.

At Fort Malate, American soldiers replace Spanish colors with the American flag after capturing the fort in August 1898.

The American government hastily organized those army forces under Gen. Wesley Merritt to defeat the Spanish army of General Jáudenes. The army, called the Eighth Army, arrived in the Philippine Islands in several groups. The ships escorting the soldiers of one of those contingents seized the Spanish island of Guam along the way. Guam then served as a coaling station for the American Eastern fleet.

Wesley Merritt

American army and navy forces near Manila completed their military preparations on August 7. Admiral Dewey and General Merritt issued a joint notice to General Jáudenes in Fort San Antonio Abad that they would attack the fortress within forty-eight hours if he did not surrender. The Spanish refused to surrender, and American operations belatedly began against Fort San Antonio Abad on August 13.

The American navy began a bombardment of Spanish fortifications in support of American army units. The Americans then attacked Spanish positions guarding the approaches to the fort. The Spanish put up only token resistance. After half an hour of bombarding the fort, American troops swept into Fort San Antonio Abad, and the American flag was soon waving over the battlefield. Six Americans had been killed, and thirty-nine were wounded. The war was over in the East.

The American people went wild over these events. George Dewey was promoted from commodore to admiral. He received a ten-thousand-dollar Tiffany sword and a house in Washington, D.C. Dewey became a national hero.

People wrote poems praising him. This one by Eugene F. Ware captures the fierce nationalism of the American people stimulated by the Battle of Manila Bay:

O Dewey was the morning
Upon the first of May
And Dewey was the Admiral
Down in Manila Bay:
And Dewey were the Regent's eyes.
Them orbs of Royal Blue!
And Dewey feel discouraged?
I do not think we Dew.

The events of the war in the East were paralleled by the military actions in the West. The United States was about to liberate Cuba.

CHAPTER SIX

The War in the Atlantic

American military planners had to solve a basic strategic problem in order to free Cuba from Spain. They had to gain control of the waters surrounding Cuba so the American army could land safely and fight the Spanish. To accomplish this, the United States had to do two things. First, it had to blockade Cuba and prevent supplies from coming to the aid of the Spanish army. The United States government declared a naval blockade of Cuba on April 21, 1898, and sent ships to patrol the waters surrounding the island.

Second, the U.S. Navy had to find and destroy the large Spanish fleet of Admiral Cervera. Once Cervera's fleet was no longer an obstacle, the American army mobilizing in Tampa could board ships, sail to Cuba, and begin the land war against the Spanish army.

The execution of these operations was put under the direction of Rear Adm. William T. Sampson, commander of the North Atlantic Fleet. Sampson divided his fleet, placing a small group of fast ships under the command of Commodore Winfield Scott Schley. Schley's group of ships was called the Flying Squadron. Its task was to seek out the Spanish ships and report their location to Sampson. Schley also patrolled the waters west of Cuba.

Most of the rest of Sampson's fleet kept up a blockade of Cuban ports while keeping a watch for Cervera's fleet. Sampson himself patrolled the waters east of Cuba and explored Caribbean ports. The navy desperately needed to locate and destroy the Spanish fleet because it posed a threat to American ports and ships. It also made it impossible to land an American army safely in Cuba.

Rear Adm. William T. Sampson, commander of the North Atlantic Fleet.

William Thomas Sampson

William Thomas Sampson (1840–1902) was commander of the North Atlantic Fleet, which finally destroyed the Spanish ships of Admiral Cervera at the battle of Santiago Harbor on July 3, 1898. The American fleet was so successful partly because navy leaders had incorporated recent scientific advances into the design of ships and their weapons. In this aspect, William Thomas Sampson was a great leader.

Sampson had a long and distinguished career in the U.S. Navy. He served a total of forty-five years, including years spent at the Naval Academy, the Navy Department, and with the fleet that was on active duty during the Civil War. He took a particular interest in the development of physics and chemistry programs at the Naval Academy and encouraged students to learn about the importance of electricity in the development of modern warships.

From 1893 until 1897, Sampson served as chief of the Bureau of Ordnance. An intelligent and courageous leader, he promoted a wide range of changes in navy defense systems. He was responsible for the adoption of an advanced form of smokeless gunpowder, for the use of electricity in operating the turrets on new battleships, and for the use of telescopic sights on ships in the modern fleet. And approximately 95 percent of the guns that were used at the battle of Santiago were made under his direction.

Sampson's dedication to the modernization of the navy and his skill with artillery made him a natural selection to lead the North Atlantic Fleet into war in 1898. Several officers senior to Sampson, including Commodore Schley, were passed over when the decision was made to put Sampson in charge. This may help to explain why Schley did not follow orders when he left the mouth of the Santiago harbor before the battle of Santiago de Cuba.

William T. Sampson promoted modern naval defense systems.

U.S. troops construct a telegraph line at Pinar del Rio, Cuba. The telegraph enabled the army to quickly relay intelligence information to and from headquarters.

The Americans knew that Cervera's fleet had left the Spanish port of Saint Vincent on April 29. But then it had disappeared from view. For two critical weeks in May, Sampson and Schley frantically searched for the fleet in the Caribbean islands and the sea lane approaches to Cuba.

Although the American navy did not know it, Cervera himself was in a terrible situation. Cervera had successfully left Spain and crossed the Atlantic. But he lacked adequate coal and food supplies. He could not locate the supply ships that had been sent ahead to meet him. So he was forced to make several landings on Caribbean islands in search of desperately needed coal and fresh food and water. These landings made it difficult for the American navy to discover his whereabouts.

Sampson and the American government assumed that Cervera's fleet would most likely land in the Cuban port of Havana. Most of the Spanish army was concentrated near Havana, and these soldiers urgently needed the weapons, ammunition, and other military supplies that Cervera carried in the holds of his ships. So the Americans kept a close watch in the waters off Havana.

But Admiral Cervera eluded the American ships patrolling Cuban waters. After making several coaling stops, the Spanish admiral arrived safely at the port of Santiago de Cuba, on the southern coast of the island, on May 19, 1898.

Winfield Scott Schley

A distinguished career naval officer, Winfield Scott Schley (1839–1911) served as the head of the Department of Modern Languages at the Naval Academy. He was appointed by Sampson to head the Flying Squadron, a group of fast and powerful cruisers whose task it was to locate the Spanish fleet under Admiral Cervera. The Flying Squadron was originally based in Hampton Roads, Virginia. The squadron included the battleships *Texas* and *Brooklyn,* and the protected cruisers *Columbia* and *Minneapolis.* The squadron's task was to be ready to fight in the Caribbean or travel to the waters off Spain to attack Spanish cities.

When Sampson received information that the Spanish fleet had been sighted, he sent orders to Schley to verify that it was in Santiago. Schley originally ignored Sampson's orders, and then later, when he did sail to Santiago, did not make a complete examination of the harbor to determine the location of the Spanish fleet. It is suspected that Schley resented Sampson's promotion to lead the North Atlantic Fleet and found it difficult to follow the orders of an officer who had been inferior to him in rank before the Spanish-American War began.

Naval officer Winfield Scott Schley headed the Flying Squadron.

The American fleet attacks the weaker Spanish fleet in Santiago, Cuba, July 1898.

It was some time before the American fleet located Admiral Cervera. Schley had been ordered to verify rumors that Cervera had arrived safely in Santiago. He arrived at the mouth of the harbor, but the approach to the inner harbor curved and Schley could not see the Spanish fleet.

Finally, it was a relatively new invention that helped the Americans locate the Spanish fleet. At the beginning of the war, President McKinley gave instructions that the telegraph company in Cuba should assist the American war effort. As a result of these instructions, an American secret agent was placed in the telegraph office in Havana.

On May 26, 1898, McKinley's foresight paid off. On that day, the secret agent spotted the Spanish fleet and sent an alarm to Washington and to Sampson's fleet that Admiral Cervera was in the Santiago harbor. Admiral Sampson's fleet immediately began to converge at the mouth of the harbor.

Admiral Cervera knew that his fleet was smaller and weaker than the American fleet. Ship bottoms were fouled from lack of proper maintenance, and most of his fleet could not outshoot or outrun the fastest of the American ships. Nonetheless, Admiral Cervera knew that his duty required sacrificing his fleet to uphold Spanish honor.

The converted yacht Gloucester *took part in the destruction of the Spanish fleet at Santiago.*

On July 3, 1898, Admiral Cervera ordered all the sailors who had been serving as soldiers in Santiago to board ship. With these reinforcements, Cervera led his flagship, the *Maria Teresa,* out of the harbor. He was followed by the *Viscaya, Cristobal Colon, Almirante Oquendo, Pluton,* and *Furor.*

Cervera's Strategy

The Spanish fleet did not want to fight. It wanted to escape. It turned west while hugging the shore. If all failed, Cervera planned to drive the ships ashore and save as many Spanish lives as possible. As the doomed fleet emerged from the harbor, it confronted the American fleet arranged in an arc around the entrance. From west to east lay the *Vixon, Brooklyn, Texas, Iowa, Oregon, Gloucester, Indiana, Erickson,* and *New York.*

The American ships raked the Spanish fleet with volleys of cannon fire. The first ship the Spanish fleet encountered at the mouth of the harbor was the *Brooklyn.* So the Spanish fleet concentrated on attacking that ship. The *Brooklyn* circled to the east, almost colliding with the *Texas,* forcing the *Texas* to swerve. It was a critical moment for both American ships, as they could have been severely damaged. Then the ships righted themselves and continued their attack on the Spanish fleet.

In spite of the extreme confusion of the American naval forces, the Spanish fleet was doomed. The wooden decks of the ships caught fire easily, and became burning infernos from which the sailors desperately tried to escape. A Spanish officer later wrote: "The fire was terrific; shells were continually striking new fire wherever they struck. Our men were driven from the guns by the rain of secondary battery projectiles, and by the flame and smoke of burning wood in our ships. The decks and the joiner work in the officers' quarters and all along the berth-deck took fire."

Many of the Spanish sailors jumped from those burning coffins and tried to swim back to shore. William Randolph Hearst was there to capture the moment. He had personally chartered a fleet of tugboats and led twenty war correspondents and artists to the scene of battle.

Now, Hearst rolled up his trousers and jumped into the water. Waving a huge revolver in his hand, he rounded up the exhausted and defeated Spanish sailors and herded them into his newspaper ships. Depictions of Hearst's own exploits filled the New York newspapers as the naval battle at Santiago Bay came to an end.

The last major naval battle of the Spanish-American War took place at Santiago, Cuba in July 1898. It resulted in an overwhelming victory for the U.S. Navy.

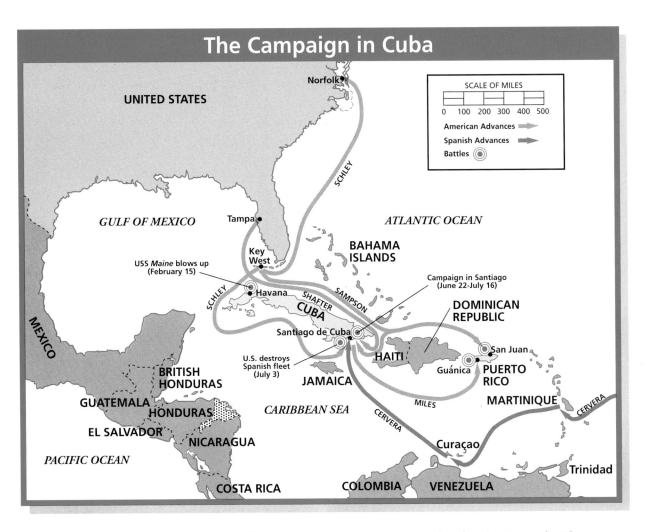

The Campaign in Cuba

That battle was a very costly affair for the Spanish. The Spanish had more than four hundred dead and wounded, and eighteen hundred Spanish sailors were captured during the naval action. The Spanish fleet was completely destroyed.

The American losses were slight. Only one American sailor lost his life during the battle. It was an overwhelming American victory and the last major naval action of the Spanish-American War.

With a touch of poetic justice, Capt. Charles D. Sigsbee, former captain of the *Maine,* participated in the battle in command of the *St. Paul.* As the battle ended, the *Oregon* slowed its furnaces and a cry of vindication rose from the throats of her seamen. "Remember the Maine!" echoed across the water.

An Easy Victory

The war at sea was over. The next day was the Fourth of July. The headlines in the New York papers read, "CERVERA'S SQUADRON DESTROYED." There would soon be more good news for Americans as the war on land progressed.

Preparations for the land war in Cuba had begun in Washington as soon as the Spanish fleet was known to be bottled up in Santiago. Originally, the United States had planned to land the American army near Havana. When news arrived that Cervera had been located and trapped in Santiago, however, American plans changed instantly. There were far fewer Spanish soldiers in Santiago than in Havana. If the American army fought at Santiago, it could use a far smaller force than had been planned.

On May 26, 1898, President McKinley and his cabinet made the decision to send sixteen thousand American soldiers to fight the Spanish army near Santiago. McKinley decided to send this army as soon as possible to end the war quickly.

The soldiers pressed into early action formed a unit called the Fifth Army Corps. It consisted of regiments from the regular army and a few volunteer units whose leaders used political connections to get to the fighting first.

The corps was under the direction of Maj. Gen. William R. Shafter. Shafter had fought in the Civil War and in the Indian wars that followed. It would have been hard to find a less impressive military figure to lead the American army, however: At three hundred pounds, Shafter was barely able to move about.

The wreck of the Spanish ship Reina Mercedes, *sunk during the fighting at Santiago.*

(above) Loaded transports head out of Tampa Bay, carrying troops and critical supplies to Cuba. (left) A cavalry bugler takes cover behind his horse. (below) The Third Cavalry in Cuba 1898.

One cynic referred to him as a "sixty-three years old gouty veteran who looked like three men rolled into one."

What made matters worse was that Shafter, like many other army officers in 1898, had no experience in leading large groups of men. For Shafter and the men under his command, fighting the Spanish-American War was truly an example of on-the-job training. General Shafter and his troops sailed from Tampa so hastily that his army was barely prepared for battle.

The Rough Riders

One of the best-known units to leave for Cuba with Shafter was a volunteer regiment called the Rough Riders. The Rough Riders were an odd assortment of ex-Confederate soldiers, old Indian fighters, New York City athletes, shopkeepers, and others.

The Rough Riders were under the command of Col. Leonard Wood. But the most famous of the group was its second in command, Lt. Col. Theodore Roosevelt. Roosevelt had resigned from his position as under secretary of the navy on the day the United States entered the war against Spain. He wanted to fight.

Roosevelt had done some fast thinking to get his Rough Riders to Cuba. Because his regiment was not a regular army unit, there was no place on board the ships leaving for Cuba for his group. Roosevelt, however, was determined to fight. He described how he managed to leave for Cuba with the first wave of soldiers:

> I ran at full speed to our train; and leaving a strong guard with the baggage I double-quicked the rest of the regiment up to the boat to board her as she came into the quay and then to hold her against the second and the seventy-first regiments which had been assigned to her.

The Fifth Corps, along with the Rough Riders, departed from Florida on June 14, 1898, with inadequate equipment, supplies, and food. Frantic arrangements had to be made to transport even these few troops to Cuba. When they arrived near Santiago, they found that almost no transport boats were available to take them from their ships to the shore. Many items were simply thrown overboard to be dragged ashore. Much of their scarce equipment and many of their pack animals were lost in the waters during the landing between June 20 and June 26.

By pushing and shoving, Roosevelt also managed to be among the first to land in Cuba: "We did the landing as we had done everything else, that is, in a scramble."

This lack of organization seemed to characterize the entire land war in Cuba. There was little coordination between the army and the navy, and the troops suffered as a result. By the end of the war, Admiral Sampson and General Shafter were barely on

Maj. Gen. William Shafter, commander of the Fifth Army Corps.

Col. Leonard Wood commanded the famous Rough Riders.

A haphazard landing of troops in Cuba. A lack of organization and poor communication between the army and navy hindered the transfer of U.S. troops and supplies to Cuba.

speaking terms. In the end, starvation among the defending Spanish troops plus their lack of ammunition and heavy guns played as great a role in the American victory as did the efforts of the poorly organized American troops.

The first military confrontation took place on June 24. An American force of about one thousand men, including the Rough Riders, forced about fifteen hundred Spanish soldiers to leave the heights above Las Guasimas. Few casualties were suffered on either side. The Spanish army withdrew almost immediately. Its commanding officer, Gen. Arsenio Linares, decided to make a stand instead at the San Juan Heights, located several miles from the outskirts of the city of Santiago de Cuba.

The American forces then attacked two separate sites located in those heights, the village of El Caney and San Juan Hill. Both were hilltop fortifications. San Juan Hill had several brick blockhouses at its summit. The blockhouses were made of thick wooden planks to withstand enemy fire. Small groups of Spanish

(above) General Shafter used fifteen thousand troops to attack the fortifications of El Caney. (right) A Spanish blockhouse. (below) Battery in action during seige of Santiago. (below right) Barbed wire entanglements near Santiago.

soldiers were well-placed at both locations to repel an attack. Both sites were within the range of the guns of the American naval forces under Admiral Sampson. The naval guns never fired.

On July 1, 1898, General Shafter ordered the infantry to charge these hills without waiting for any artillery fire to weaken the Spanish fortifications. A British newspaper reporter on the scene described San Juan Hill: "But this hill—the look of it was enough to stagger any man. Was this to be taken practically without the aid of artillery? Artillery should have battered and battered and battered the position and then the infantry might have swept up at the run. The infantry stood before the thing alone."

The order was given to charge at both locations. The Spanish were outnumbered at El Caney 12 to 1, on San Juan Hill 16 to 1. But before the day was over, it was clear that the American army had underestimated the military skill of the Spanish soldiers. American losses totaled 1,385; 205 dead and 1,180 wounded. Spanish losses were 215 killed, 376 wounded, and 2 taken prisoner for a total of 593. Although this was much less than the American total, the casualties amounted to approximately half the Spanish defenders who had fought at both battle sites. They had made a heroic stand. During the fighting, General Linares was seriously wounded and had to be replaced by Gen. Jose Toral.

(left) New York volunteers in the trenches at San Juan Hill. (below) A Spanish blockhouse at Cumanayagua, Cuba. The brick walls and narrow rifle windows made this type of blockhouse difficult to capture.

The Campaign in Santiago

El Caney (July 1)

Surrender (July 17)

Santiago de Cuba

San Juan Hill (July 1)

Las Guasimas (June 24)

CERVERA

Sinking of USS *Merrimac* (June 3)

SAMPSON

SCHLEY

CERVERA

SHAFTER

Daiquiri

Siboney

CARIBBEAN SEA

SCALE OF MILES

0   4

American Advances ➤
Spanish Advances ➤
Battles ◉

Reckless Acts of Heroism

There were also many American heroes that day. But it was Theodore Roosevelt's recklessly brave antics that captured the imagination of the American public on July 1, 1898. Richard Harding Davis, a famous newspaper reporter, accompanied the Rough Riders and reported on the doings of Terrible Teddy.

As historian Margaret Leech observed, there was something heroic about the "bespectacled volunteer soldier, a blue polka-dotted handkerchief flowing from his sombrero, charging the enemy earth works at the head of his men. The image was grand enough to gain him the presidency."

Despite these heroics, General Shafter was horrified by the casualties among the American soldiers and by the yellow fever that was beginning to strike his troops. Richard Harding Davis described the suffering for the American reading public: "Men gasped on their back, like fishes in the bottom of a boat, their heads burning inside and out, their limbs too heavy to move. They had been rushed here and there wet with sweat and wet with fording the streams, under a sun that would have made moving a fan an effort, and they lay prostrate, gasping at the hot air, with faces aflame, and their tongues sticking out, and their eyes rolling." Instead of attacking Santiago de Cuba immediately after the victories on July 1, General Shafter decided to seal off the city from supplies and then use artillery to bombard it.

The Spanish faced a hopeless situation. The countryside surrounding the besieged city was controlled by Cuban rebel forces. Admiral Cervera's fleet was destroyed on July 3, so there was no hope that the desperate Spanish army could escape by sea.

(above) A painting of the wild-eyed Rough Riders led by Theodore Roosevelt. (right) The Rough Riders pose for a photograph.

General Toral's troops waited for either attack or starvation.

On July 4 and again on July 10, Shafter demanded the surrender of Toral's troops. American artillery shelled the city, where water supplies had almost disappeared. Finally, the Spanish agreed to negotiations on July 11, and a surrender agreement was signed on July 16. The conditions of the agreement stated that the Spanish would leave Santiago, that Spanish officers would be allowed to carry their sidearms, and that Spanish soldiers would be returned to Spain at American expense. On July 17, Spanish forces occupying Santiago de Cuba marched out of the town.

The military actions at Santiago convinced the Spanish government that Cuba was lost. And the Spanish government was satisfied that the troops under the command of Generals Linares and Toral had fought bravely. Cuba would be free. But the American people and leaders of the army were not satisfied.

One week after the surrender of General Toral, another American general got an opportunity to participate in the war. On July 24, 1898, the president ordered Maj. Gen. Nelson A. Miles to begin an attack on the Spanish island colony of Puerto Rico. Once the United States entered the war with Spain, American leaders took the opportunity to fight for and take as many Spanish colonies as possible. Between July 25 and August 11, Miles all but completed the conquest of the island. The campaign was so rapid that the newspapers referred to it as "General Miles' Gran' Picnic and Moonlight Excursion in Puerto Rico." The Spanish garrison on the island did not resist strongly. Because the United States had been victorious in Cuba, the Spanish expected them to win again.

The Spanish-American War was almost over. On August 12, 1898, in Madrid, representatives of the United States and Spain signed an agreement to end hostilities. They would shortly meet in Paris to draw up a peace treaty. Unfortunately, news of this understanding did not reach Manila, in the Philippine Islands, until after American forces stormed the Spanish fortress on August 15, 1898.

Maj. Gen. Nelson A. Miles led the U.S. attack on Puerto Rico.

American soldiers celebrate after hearing that the Spanish have surrendered at Santiago.

(above) The principal wharf in Puerto Rico. (right) A huge cannon guards the harbor at San Juan. (below) The Spanish garrison occupying Puerto Rico offered only token resistance to Maj. Gen. Miles's forces.

On December 10, 1898, Spanish and U.S. representatives meet in Paris to sign a peace treaty.

An Overwhelming Success

This final victory meant that the United States had been successful on all battlefronts. And although Americans merely took
advantage of the weakened state of the Spanish military, the
American people themselves knew little about these weaknesses.
They believed the United States had beaten a strong world
power. The American newspapers emphasized the victories, and
the readers began to believe their country was a great military
power.

CHAPTER SEVEN

Results of the War

The United States emerged from the Spanish-American War with a great deal more than American leaders expected. At war's end, the United States controlled Puerto Rico and Cuba in the Caribbean Sea and Guam and the Philippine Islands in the Pacific Ocean.

Representatives of the United States and Spain then went to Paris to discuss peace terms. There, the United States demanded complete freedom for Cuba. It also demanded political control over the islands it had conquered during the war.

Spain had no choice but to agree to these terms. The American demands were incorporated in the Treaty of Paris that was signed by representatives of Spain and the United States on December 10, 1898. The Treaty of Paris marked the end of Spanish control of a once-great empire. It simultaneously marked the emergence of the United States as an imperial power, a country that controls the domestic and foreign affairs of other people.

As a result of the war, the United States took on an important role in managing the affairs of the western hemisphere. One of its goals was to keep the influence of European powers out of the region. During the nineteenth century, the United States produced the Monroe Doctrine but did not have the power to enforce it. In the aftermath of the Spanish-American War, the Monroe Doctrine became the guiding principle of U.S. foreign policy. And the United States could enforce its beliefs with a military force that was ready to fight.

The war also resulted in U.S. plans to build a canal linking the Atlantic and Pacific oceans across the country of Panama.

One event during the Spanish-American War had indicated the need for such a canal. This was the spectacular voyage of the battleship *Oregon*.

The ship had been docked in Puget Sound, off the coast of Washington State, at the beginning of the crisis. It made the heroic sea voyage around the tip of South America and arrived in Key West, Florida, on May 26, in time to take part in the blockade of Cuba. That thirteen-thousand mile voyage took the *Oregon* sixty-five days to complete. If a canal connecting the Atlantic and Pacific had existed, the trip would have been completed in one-third the time.

Supporters of an American canal used the voyage of the *Oregon* to support their campaign. They believed the canal would be a useful route during times of war and also an important trade route during peacetime. Chief among those supporters was Theodore Roosevelt, who became president of the United States

(left) War refugees from Santiago, Cuba. (below) The Third Field Artillery near Ponce, Puerto Rico, after gaining control of the island. At war's end, the United States controlled Puerto Rico.

The Panama Canal

People had long dreamed of finding a way of connecting the Atlantic and Pacific oceans through Central America by means of a canal. A French company, organized by the famous builder of the Suez Canal, Ferdinand de Lesseps, began work on such a canal in 1879. The project failed because of financial difficulties and because many workers died from tropical diseases. Before the Spanish-American War, the United States had also considered the possibility of building a canal in conjunction with Great Britain. After the war, the United States wanted the project to be an entirely American undertaking.

This change in attitude toward the canal came about as a result of events during the war. During the fighting, American military planners realized the importance of being able to move ships quickly between the Atlantic and the Pacific oceans. On its way to becoming an imperial power, the United States did not want to share control of the canal with another country. So American leaders decided to develop the canal themselves.

Engineers suggested that the best route for a canal lay across Panama, then part of Colombia. The Colombian government decided not to sign a treaty with the United States to sell the land for the project. At that point, some Panamanians decided to declare their independence from Colombia. The American government supported the revolt of Panama against Colombia in 1903 and quickly granted political recognition of the new country. The United States then negotiated a treaty with Panama that permitted the construction of a canal. It also granted the United States a ninety-nine-year lease of a ten-mile-wide zone surrounding the canal in exchange for a yearly rental fee of $250,000 a year.

The American government was able to negotiate a treaty with Panama to build the Panama Canal. The United States wanted sole control of the strategic canal.

Theodore Roosevelt became the U.S. president following the Spanish-American War.

in 1901. As president, Roosevelt began a lively campaign to alert the American people to the importance of a canal for military security. Roosevelt took an active role in assisting Panama, then a possession of Colombia, in gaining its independence in 1901. He then received permission to begin construction of a canal across the Isthmus of Panama, which connected North and South America. The efforts of Roosevelt and his supporters resulted in the opening of the enormously important ship canal linking the Atlantic and Pacific oceans in 1911. In future wars, the United States could move its troops around the world with greater speed.

Improving the Military

Construction of the Panama Canal was one of the many changes that resulted in a more powerful United States. Another of these changes—the establishment of a general military staff—affected the ability of the United States to wage a future war.

American military leaders realized that the country had won its first conflict with a European power only because of the enemy's weakness. These leaders knew that a war with another major country would have ended in defeat for the U.S. Army. There was an urgent need for a change in its organization. The Congress therefore began the development of a general staff.

A general staff acts as the brain of an army by directing, planning, and organizing all of the army's activities. Since the American

Hawaii

The Hawaiian Islands lie in the Pacific Ocean, many thousands of miles from the coast of the United States. They were discovered by Capt. James Cook, a British explorer, in the 1780s and were long used by American shippers and whalers as a resting place on voyages. Many New Englanders decided to stay on the islands, and their settlements looked like small New England villages.

The sugar plantations were the source of the islands' wealth. Americans controlled the sugar-growing industry in Hawaii, and the native Polynesian people worked on the plantations, harvesting the sugarcane. In addition, in 1887, the United States obtained exclusive use of Pearl Harbor from Hawaii. Pearl Harbor served as a valuable naval station for the new steel navy.

In 1893, annexationists in the United States failed to convince Congress that the government should take control of the Hawaiian Islands. In 1898, however, taking advantage of the imperial spirit that accompanied the Spanish-American War, annexationists gained the ear of President McKinley, who actively urged the annexation of Hawaii. Hawaii was annexed and the native ruler, Queen Liliuokalani, was overthrown in 1898.

The U.S. government annexed Hawaii in 1898, largely because of its strategic mid-Pacific location.

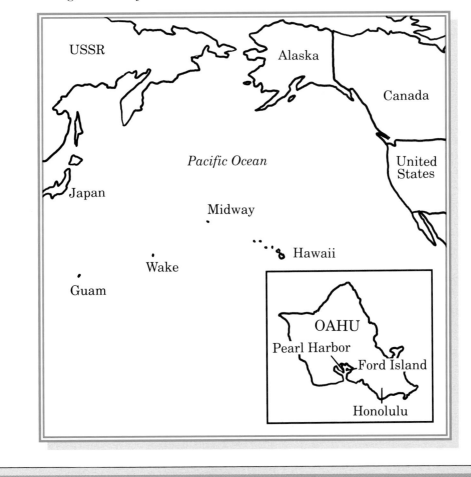

people had feared the existence of any kind of standing army in peacetime, the United States was almost the only major country without a general staff. The consequence was the confusion in all branches of the national service, which had been painfully clear during the training and equipping of the troops at Tampa.

That confusion altered the attitude of the American people toward the development of an efficient military force. The first piece of legislation that resulted in the creation of a general staff was signed by Congress in 1903. The staff was in place by the beginning of World War I. When the United States entered that war in 1917, American soldiers at the front did not suffer from the same problems that afflicted the troops in 1898.

The Spanish-American War also brought about some changes in how Americans viewed the countries of Europe. The change in attitude toward Great Britain was the most dramatic. Until the end of the nineteenth century, Great Britain was disliked and distrusted by the people of the United States. This negative attitude was the result of the antagonism felt for the British during the Revolutionary War, the War of 1812, and during the American Civil War, when Great Britain aided the Confederacy. The behavior of Great Britain during the Spanish-American War helped to change this attitude.

The United States and Great Britain

During the Spanish-American War, Great Britain was the sole European power that sided with the United States. All the others openly befriended Spain. Only Great Britain was, in the phrase of historian Samuel Eliot Morison, "ready to cheer America down the path of imperialism." Great Britain's leaders encouraged the United States to take military action against the Spanish forces on the Philippine Islands and openly supported the American decision to keep the islands as imperial possessions at the conclusion of the war.

This staunch support for the United States ended the anti-British feelings in the youthful country. It led to the beginning of a mature friendship that has endured through many wars and that remains today.

On the other hand, events during the war led to the development of poor relations with Germany. German leaders did not like the fact that the United States was gaining an empire while Germany's foreign holdings remained small.

Soon after Admiral Dewey's great victory, German battleships appeared at Manila Bay. They attempted to interfere with American military operations. According to one newspaper, the Germans were there "not to protect existing German interests but to find new interests to protect." The bad feelings Americans had for Germany continued long after the end of the Spanish-American

War. Dislike of Germany contributed to strong anti-German feelings at the beginning of World War I.

All of these changes were significant. They led to the development of a new view toward the rest of the world on the part of the United States.

During the nineteenth century, the United States had been content to look after its own interests. Most people wanted only to expand the country's frontiers to the Pacific Ocean. Now, with the development of the new steel navy and a growing army, the United States began to feel more self-assured. It saw itself as the guardian of the undeveloped countries it had acquired and as the natural protector of the peoples of South America.

That feeling led the country to annex Hawaii. The United States had long had a connection with the Pacific island chain and by the end of the nineteenth century, American sugarcane growers controlled the islands' economy. Now that the United States controlled the Philippine Islands and began to contemplate trade with China, Hawaii's harbors would be an important naval asset. So on July 7, 1898, Congress annexed the islands during the heat of the Spanish-American War.

A New Sense of National Unity

On the mainland, equally dramatic changes took place in the wake of the Spanish-American War. One of these was the development of a sense of national unity that had previously been shattered by the Civil War. In the minds of many Americans, the Civil War did not really end until the Spanish-American War. This was because until the 1890s, many people, particularly people in the South, were still divided by Civil War memories.

After 1865, many Northerners moved to the South and treated Southerners as if they were a conquered people. This domination of the political and economic affairs of the South left deep scars and anger between the two sections of the country. In many ways, North and South remained divided until 1898.

The Spanish-American War gave Northerners and Southerners a common enemy to hate. They stopped hating each other so they could cooperate in fighting Spain. This change was reflected in the difference in treatment given to the Sixth Massachusetts Regiment in 1861 and then in 1898. During the war in 1861, soldiers of the regiment were stoned as they passed through the Southern city of Baltimore on their way to war. But in 1898, hostilities had lessened so much that when this same military unit stopped near the capital on its way to Tampa, it was treated to a massive reception in Washington. One writer announced that the reception was "the most dramatic event of the war on American soil for it was not a mere reception and patriotic demonstration. It was the new national spirit rising Phoenix-like from the ashes of '61."

A Civil War soldier holds a tattered Union flag. Historians feel that the Spanish-American War brought a unifying spirit to the nation, finally healing the old wounds of the Civil War.

President McKinley contributed greatly to this spiritual union of the nation. He selected generals from both Civil War armies to lead the units in Cuba. Former Confederate cavalry hero Joe Wheeler led a unit that fought near Santiago. When he was selected for service, Wheeler announced proudly that "a single battle for the Union flag was worth fifteen years of life." These were unusual words coming from the mouth of a Confederate officer who had spent more than four years trying to destroy the Union.

Northerners and Southerners served with great pride during the Spanish-American War. Their enthusiasm and love of country found expression in this poem by William Lightfoot Visscher:

Blue and Grey are One
Hurrah for the East and the West!
The nation is one, individual and free,
And all of its sons are the best.

Black soldiers in a U.S. training camp. Four regular army black regiments fought in Cuba. For the first time in U.S. history, black officers led them into battle.

Blacks and Whites

The Spanish-American War not only helped to overcome regional differences but also influenced relations between blacks and whites. The Civil War had freed the slaves, but it did not free people's minds of prejudice. The Spanish-American War was an opportunity for the country to move toward this goal.

There were four black regiments in the U.S. Army in 1898. The chaplain of one of these regiments, the Twenty-fifth Infantry, expressed the opinion of many black people when he said, "I believe that this war will very greatly help the American colored man of the South, and result in the further clearing of the national atmosphere."

Many American blacks showed their patriotism. In addition to the four regular army regiments, eight to ten thousand black men volunteered to serve in 1898. But they were still not integrated into the regular forces.

While the black volunteers, like most of the white volunteers, spent the war in American training camps, the experience of the regular army soldiers was very different. The four regular black regiments were involved in the fighting in Cuba. For the very first time in American history, these black soldiers served under the command of black officers.

Walter Reed

Physician and educator Walter Reed (1851–1902) was a famous U.S. bacteriologist, a scientist who studies one-celled microorganisms. Such organisms can be seen only with the aid of a microscope.

Walter Reed served in the U.S. Army for many years as a military surgeon. He became interested in bacteriology and especially in the study of epidemic diseases as a result of his treatment of soldiers during the Spanish-American War.

The American troops preparing to fight in Cuba in 1898 were affected by diseases such as typhoid, and Reed worked to reduce the effects of this particular outbreak. It was at this time that he became very interested in the deadly disease known as yellow jack or yellow fever.

He made the discovery that the disease was carried by a mosquito (*Stegomyia fasciata*) and not caused by contact with body fluids or soiled clothing, as many people believed.

Walter Reed discovered that a mosquito contracted the disease by biting an infected person. In turn, the infected mosquito transmitted yellow fever by biting another person. The bite transmitted the disease into the bloodstream. Knowledge of how the disease spread enabled the United States, Cuba, and many countries in Latin America to begin to tackle the dreaded killer. Countries started extermination programs to eliminate the mosquito and yellow fever, which had been a deadly problem for hundreds of years.

Walter Reed discovered that bites from infected mosquitoes could transmit disease.

Nurses and convalescent patients at Camp Thomas, Georgia.

The Ninth and Tenth Cavalry and the Twenty-fourth and Twenty-fifth Infantry units were sent to Tampa. They became an important part of the Fifth Army Corps, which fought in Cuba. They showed great valor at El Caney and at San Juan Hill, where their military abilities were noted by Theodore Roosevelt. The four black regiments served with great distinction in 1898 and were a credit to their country.

The people of the United States also benefited from the war in other ways. For example, there were many major advances in sanitation and medical treatments. Knowledge gained in the training camps led to better ways of disposing of and treating waste to prevent infection. Also, the Army Medical Corps was greatly enlarged as a result of the enormous medical deficiencies experienced during the Spanish-American War. In future conflicts, soldiers would receive quicker and better treatment.

Walter Reed

The most dramatic advances in the medical field were made by Maj. Walter Reed and his associates in the Army Medical Corps. Before the Spanish-American War, no one knew that the bite of an infected mosquito caused yellow fever. Reed and his staff conducted experiments in Cuba that led to this revolutionary discovery. His work with the *Stegomyia* mosquito led to the destruction of the mosquitoes' breeding grounds. As a result, yellow fever gradually ceased to be a problem.

Mass outbreaks of yellow fever had halted several attempts in the 1870s and 1880s to build a canal linking the Atlantic and Pacific oceans. Thousands of workers had died from the disease. Thanks to Reed, it became possible to build a canal in mosquito-infested Panama by destroying the breeding grounds of the insects.

Advances in medicine were not the only changes the war brought. Significant changes also took place in the field of politics. The role of the presidency, for example, was altered during the Spanish-American War. Many of McKinley's immediate predecessors had been colorless men, and the office of the presidency was in decline at the end of the nineteenth century. Several previous presidents had been elected only because of their Civil War experience. These presidents did very little for the country during their terms. William McKinley assumed responsibilities that many presidents had ignored in the past. McKinley was interested in and played a vital role in foreign affairs. Other presidents had been content to let Congress conduct foreign policy. He was

The Spanish-American War established the United States as a world power. When Woodrow Wilson became president in 1913, he was able to expand American foreign power because of the nation's enhanced credibility.

assisted by technological advances that enabled him to exercise an effective, direct control never before possible.

McKinley had originally opposed the war, but once he understood the national mood, he stepped out to lead. He actively directed the war effort, filling in when his subordinates proved to be incompetent. Originally an anti-expansionist, McKinley came to believe that it was important for the United States to have an empire. So the president took his message to Congress and to the American people. He even went on several major speaking tours in order to gain support for this position. He made expansionism an acceptable principle of U.S. foreign policy.

William McKinley gave new life to the office of the presidency and set an example of activism for his successors. The outspoken and aggressive behavior of Theodore Roosevelt and the plunge into foreign matters taken by Woodrow Wilson were more easily accepted by the American public as a result of McKinley's work during the Spanish-American War.

These various developments were among the most significant consequences of the short war that the United States fought with Spain in 1898. Both domestically and in foreign affairs, great changes took place. The country could not return to its earlier, carefree attitude toward world matters. It had entered the ranks of the world's great powers. America was called upon to accept new responsibilities. During World War I, the United States emerged as the most important military and political power in the world.

For Further Reading

Jack DeMattos, *Masterson & Roosevelt*. College Station, TX: Creative Texas, 1984.

Eden Force, *Theodore Roosevelt*. New York: Franklin Watts Inc., 1987.

Zachary Kent, *The Story of the Sinking of the Battleship* Maine. Chicago: Childrens Press, 1988.

Don Lawson, *The United States in the Spanish-American War.* New York: Abelard-Schuman, 1976.

Lou Sabin, *Teddy Roosevelt, Rough Rider.* Mahwah, NJ: Troll Associates, 1985.

The Spanish-American War Soldier at San Juan Hill. North Mankato, MN: Capstone Press, 1989.

John R. Spears, *Our Navy in the War with Spain.* New York: Charles Scribners Sons, 1898.

Rebecca Stefoff, *Theodore Roosevelt: 26th President of the United States*. Ada, OK: Garret Educational Corp., 1984.

Henry Watterson, *History of the Spanish-American War.* Chicago: H. J. Small Publishing Co., 1898.

Works Consulted

Howard K. Beale, *Theodore Roosevelt and the Rise of America to World Power*. New York: Collier Books, 1956.

Elbert J. Benton, *International Law and the Diplomacy of the Spanish-American War*. Baltimore: The Johns Hopkins Press, 1908.

Oliver Carlson, *Hearst, Lord of San Simeon*. New York: Viking Press, 1936.

George R. Clark, *A Short History of the United States Navy*. Philadelphia: J.B. Lippincott, 1911.

Lewis L. Gould, *The Presidency of William McKinley*. Lawrence: The Regents Press of Kansas, 1980.

Ferdinand Lundberg, *Imperial Hearst, a Social Biography*. New York: Equinox Cooperative Press, 1936.

Alden March, *The History and Conquest of the Philippines and Our Other Possessions*. New York: Arno Press, 1970.

Gregory Mason, *Remember the Maine*. New York: Henry Holt, 1939.

Allan Nevins and Henry Steele Commager, *A Pocket History of the United States*. New York: Washington Square Press, 1976.

Julius Pratt, *Expansionists*. Gloucester, MA: Peter Smith, 1959.

John R. Spears, *Our Navy in the War with Spain*. New York: Charles Scribners Sons, 1898.

David F. Trash, *The War with Spain in 1898*. New York: MacMillan Publishing Co., 1981.

Herbert W. Wilson, *The Downfall of Spain*. New York: Burt Franklin, 1900.

John K. Winkler, *Hearst, an American Phenomenon*. New York: Simon & Schuster, 1928.

James R. Young, *History of Our War with Spain*. Washington, DC: Library of Congress, 1898.

Index

Photo Credits

Cover photo: Library of Congress

The Bettmann Archive, 16, 92

Fish, Hamilton, by Charles Fenderich, National Portrait Gallery, Smithsonian Institution, 17 (right)

Library of Congress, 17 (left), 20, 21, 22, 24 (top), 32 (both), 33, 36, 38, 39, 40 (both), 45, 50, 51, 62, 63, 65 (top 2), 68, 71, 74, 75, 81 (top), 83 (top), 86 (top), 87 (top), 89, 93, 99, 101

National Archives, 12, 23, 24 (bottom), 25, 29, 31, 47 (both), 49, 52 (all), 53 (all), 54, 55 (left), 56, 57, 58, 61 (both), 64, 65 (bottom), 66, 67, 69, 73, 76, 77, 79, 80 (all), 82, 83 (bottom three), 84 (both), 86 (bottom), 87 (bottom), 88 (all), 91 (both), 97, 98, 100

Courtesy of the New York Historical Society, New York City, 13, 14, 35, 55 (right)

Sampson, William T., by Kurz and Allison, National Portrait Gallery, Smithsonian Institution, 72

Sherman, John, by Henry Ulke, National Portrait Gallery, Smithsonian Institution, 42 (left)

Wood, Leonard, by Johnson, National Portrait Gallery, Smithsonian Institution, 81 (bottom)

About the Author

Deborah Bachrach was born and raised in New York City, where she received her undergraduate education. She earned a Ph.D. in history from the University of Minnesota. Dr. Bachrach has taught at the University of Minnesota as well as at St. Francis College, Joliet, Illinois, and Queens College, the City University of New York. In addition, she has worked for many years in the fields of medical research and public policy development.